Keeping the Ink Wet

Keeping the Ink Wet

What the Theater Can Teach the Church About Worship

Kevin G. Yell

Foreword by Nick Wagner

RESOURCE *Publications* • Eugene, Oregon

KEEPING THE INK WET
What the Theater Can Teach the Church About Worship

Copyright © 2025 Kevin G. Yell. All rights reserved. Except for brief quotations in critical publications or reviews, no part of this book may be reproduced in any manner without prior written permission from the publisher. Write: Permissions, Wipf and Stock Publishers, 199 W. 8th Ave., Suite 3, Eugene, OR 97401.

Resource Publications
An Imprint of Wipf and Stock Publishers
199 W. 8th Ave., Suite 3
Eugene, OR 97401

www.wipfandstock.com

PAPERBACK ISBN: 979-8-3852-2818-8
HARDCOVER ISBN: 979-8-3852-2819-5
EBOOK ISBN: 979-8-3852-2820-1
VERSION NUMBER 01/02/25

Scripture quotations are taken from the New Revised Standard Version Updated Edition. Copyright © 2021 National Council of Churches of Christ in the United States of America. Used by permission. All rights reserved worldwide.

Extracts from the *Daily Meditations* of Fr. Richard Rohr OFM of the Center for Action and Contemplation (CAC) are used by permission of CAC. All rights reserved worldwide. Copyright © 2023.

Extract from *Busted Halo* website and blog of January 12, 2010 (www.bustedhalo.com) by Fr. Richard Malloy, SJ, used with permission.

Contents

Foreword by Nick Wagner | vii
Acknowledgments | ix
Introduction | xi
Prologue | xix

1. Getting Cast: Or Is It Miscast?? | 1
2. Meeting the Director and Production Team, and Beginning to Explore the Script | 15
3. Knowing, Staying In, and Not Losing Yourself in Your Role (or Archetype) | 25
4. The Historical and Cultural Context of the Script: Understanding the Roles of the Dramaturge and Liturgist | 46
5. Communication, Relationship, Change: The Theory and Consequence of How Words Have Meaning Between People | 64
6. Words in my Body: Breath, Movement, Silence and Stillness | 79
7. The Role of the Audience/Community as Critics and Sustainers | 99
8. Tech Week: Set Design, Music, Lighting, Sound, Costumes | 116
9. Knowing and Delivering Your Lines | 133
10. Dress Rehearsal and Opening Night, and the Joy and Monotony of a Long Run | 151

Epilogue | 163
Appendix | 171
Bibliography | 179

Foreword

I first met Kevin Yell thirty-ish years ago, when I was planning a conference to help parish volunteers and leaders provide more engaging worship experiences for their communities. As we brainstormed ideas, Kevin offered a suggestion that left me both unsettled and intrigued: "What if we created a conference with no lectures?" It was a radical idea, one that reflects Kevin's innovative spirit and his passion for pushing boundaries in worship and liturgy.

That same spirit of creativity and challenge permeates every page of his new book, "Keeping the Ink Wet." Kevin draws on his deep experience in both theater and liturgy to propose a fresh and dynamic approach to leading worship. He invites us to see the work of liturgical leadership—preaching, presiding, and crafting worship experiences—as akin to the art of theater and performance.

What can liturgical planners, preachers, and presiders learn from actors and directors? Quite a lot, as Kevin demonstrates through both practical examples and profound reflections. He takes us through the process of staging a theatrical production, revealing how every step—from casting to closing night—offers valuable lessons for anyone called to lead worship.

At the heart of Kevin's approach is the idea that we must view liturgy as though the ink "is always still wet." This powerful image reminds us that worship is not a static ritual bound by tradition alone but a living, breathing encounter that requires our full engagement, creativity, and responsiveness. This approach helps us remain open to new possibilities and adapt each liturgy to speak directly to the unique needs and hopes of our communities.

In a rapidly changing world, where cultural shifts demand fresh responses, Kevin's book offers helpful guidance. He equips church leaders with the skills and vision to create vibrant, meaningful worship experiences that resonate with parish communities. While deeply rooted in his own experiences, the principles Kevin presents are relevant across all liturgical traditions.

Whether you are a seasoned liturgical leader, a new preacher, or someone training others for this vital ministry, "Keeping the Ink Wet" provides both inspiration and practical tools to deepen your craft. Kevin Yell challenges us to rethink what it means to lead worship—to see each liturgy as an opportunity to create something truly transformative and alive.

I encourage you to read this book with an open mind and a willing heart. Let Kevin's insights inspire you to keep your own ink wet, to be bold in your approach, and to continually seek new ways to engage your community in worship that is as dynamic and life-giving as the God we serve.

Nick Wagner

Acknowledgments

STUDENTS NEED TEACHERS, NOVICES need mentors, and practitioners need colleagues. I have been blessed with all three over the decades, some of whom are now also friends. Most important were those who were willing to share the risk of failure by trusting a newbie with different ideas. Immense thanks and praise for courage, therefore, first go to teachers and mentors back in the UK: Jennifer Sandler (and The Epiphany Dancers,) Shiela Fairbanks (with The Interpreters and Radius, The Religious Drama Society,) along with Reverends James Brand, Edward Matthews, Donald Reeves, and Michael Shaw.

Coming to America, I was incredibly fortunate to study at The Graduate Theological Union in Berkeley, California, at a time (1991–93) when the likes of Margie Brown, Cynthia Winton Henry, Nancy Chinn, Sandra Schneiders IHM, James Emperor SJ, John Baldovin SJ, Kenan Osbourne OFM and L. William Countryman were all teaching and modeling best practices. Alongside these, Fathers Gerry O'Rourke and Robert Rien invited me to join their respective pastoral teams and learn more "on the job."

This book became a reality thanks to the support and patience of many, but especially Sharon Casey OP, and Peggy Flynn, mentors, colleagues and wonderful friends, along with my husband, Bud Bowen. Skilled editorial work by Jason D. Pettus and Virginia Kincaid formed it as a reading document rather than a flow of consciousness, and comments from Sharon Casey, Ed Wales and Michael Mansfield, all challenged me to be clear about the language I wanted to use. Matthew Wimer and George Callihan at Wipf & Stock expertly guided me through the publication process, and their patience is immense.

Finally, thanks to Nick Wagner for his Foreword and for trusting that being an artist is the most natural route for engaging the Divine child of God within each of us, even if it sometimes makes a little mess in the process.

Kevin Yell

Introduction

A CLEAR DIFFERENCE EXISTS between being an actor on a stage and a presider at an altar, between the function of a play and an act of worship. Yet there's a huge similarity in both the skills needed to do all these as well as the communal purpose intended. Why? Because the work in all these cases is to take a script which only exists on paper and turn it into a living, breathing experience.

The work—and it most certainly is real work—of the performer, preacher, and presider is to lead a community of more-or-less strangers into an experience which is outside normal space and time, and into the unknown liminal reality that the ancient Greeks called *Kairos*, "time outside time." It's why we go to the theater, and what children do every time they play. It's also what "going to church" is meant to achieve too, for every service is meant to be a "moment of heaven on earth."

In this liminal space and time, the imagination is encouraged, creativity is engaged, and the impossible becomes real. The job is to create a safe space where people can risk disengaging from the dominant priorities we (erroneously?) call "reality," and enter a place where wonder, true joy, awe, and revelation can happen. It's a space unconstrained by bank accounts, health status, or family situation, but defined by hope, healing and, most importantly, catharsis.

The job of we performers, preachers, and presiders is not to have the experience ourselves (though we might), but to do everything possible to ensure that our respective community can. One of the big differences between us, however, is that performers see their script or manuscript as a starting point. Too often church ministers see their script as an end point. I hope we can invite you to change that opinion.

As liturgical churches across the Western world empty and close, the verdict is in on the tradition where Christian clergy and lay liturgical leaders are instructed only to "say the black and do the red." (The black ink was for the minister's part, the red was for the rubrics, which are directions about where and how to stand, what to do with your hands, etc.) This directive echoes ancient theatrical, highly stylized traditions such as Noh, Kabuki, and Bunraku, where the actor must remove their individuality and personality from their role. These traditions can certainly still work well in certain circumstances, because the script and the action were invented together. When we enter these worlds, we know the rules and we live within those expectations.

However, contemporary life, both theatrical and spiritual, has a very different script and style. Christianity confirms this with an invitation to be incarnate and enculturated, to be "of the people" in the style of Jesus. To prepare liturgical leaders to do this, we urgently need new skills and training.

The human draw to ritual is almost as old as our known communal history; but the role of ritual leader needs not just to be rooted in historical experience, but also to be attuned to contemporary vision and energy, words which would have made little sense to most people 60 or so years ago. Today, Millennials live in a culturally different world from Boomers, and both are waiting to discover what the under-15 "Generation Alpha" folk are going to make of it all. We used to measure culture in centuries; now we measure it in a decade or two.

In order to help, this book is an invitation to take a journey outside the box of "church studies" and into the black box or empty space of the performing arts. A "black box" or "empty space" is what a theater team begins with every time they conceive of bringing a play to the stage. In this sense, every production begins like the book of Genesis: In the beginning there is a formless void. *The Empty Space* is also the title of a small but powerful book by the legendary theater and film director Peter Brook, who worked with, among others, The Royal Shakespeare Company and The Royal Opera House of London. Everything Brook says about theater and its practitioners in *The Empty Space* can be said about a church's services and its ministers.

We will explore the process of theater and apply it to the liturgical acts of planning, presiding and preaching in liturgy so that, like a new production of Shakespeare's *Hamlet* or a new performance of one of Bach's cello concerti, we can, in the words of St. Augustine, learn how to take something that is ever ancient and help people see it as ever new.

In the context of this book, when we talk about "words on a page" we're also talking about the notes on a staff for a musician, and the choreographic notations for a dancer. In the same way, when we talk in this book about an "actor," we can easily substitute "musician" or "dancer." If the reader feels more attuned to one or the other, then you are welcome to transpose the word.

A WORD ABOUT CHURCH WORDS

Whatever languages Jesus spoke, and he probably spoke some of at least two or three, none were English. This might seem obvious, but it never hurts to be reminded, especially if one doesn't have a facility with first century Aramaic, Hebrew, Greek or Latin, as I admit I don't. We also need to remember that the oldest written texts we have about Jesus (others probably existed but, so far, are lost,) start with some of the writings of St. Paul, who never met the historical Jesus, let alone heard him speak. Luckily for us, Jesus came from an oral tradition where stories were often learned by heart and retold over and over. We, therefore, must trust that early oral tradition to have delivered to the first gospel writers the words on which we now rely. And again, just to be clear, they weren't in English.

As if this weren't enough, we must also admit that, while Jesus was often very direct about some things his followers are called to do, (feed the poor, welcome the stranger, heal the sick. Mt. 25:31–46) he was not good about explaining more about his God, heaven or what "conquering death" really means. He gave us images, like a woman searching for a lost coin, (Lk.15:8–10) or a father welcoming home a prodigal son (Lk. 15:11–32,) like a wedding banquet but with a dress code (Mt.22:1–14,) or a sub-division with many unique houses (Jn.14:2–6.) And his images (retold through the cultural lenses of the writers,) are not always consistent across our four main gospels, which is not helpful!

His use of language in this way, (whichever one it was,) continued into the story of what we call the Last Supper, and which gives us the central Christian celebration of the Lord's Supper, sometimes also called the Eucharist (Greek for "Thanksgiving,") or Mass, (from *missa*, Latin for "sent.") Just like when talking about God or heaven, Jesus did not leave any further explanation for his words concerning the bread at the beginning of the meal being his body, nor the wine at the end being his blood. Some ask: "Did he say "is"? Did he say "like"? Did he say "becomes"?" We may not know for certain, but well over fifty different biblical translations (including all the popular ones,) translate the words as "this *is* my body," so that's the view we'll take here.[1]

Whatever Jesus said or meant, the early church knew it was very important, and they remembered it and retold the story. As the early church expanded beyond Palestine, it encountered different cultures and languages, plus different ways of using language. This gave rise to disagreements about meaning and then to various ecumenical church councils over the next seven centuries, each trying to get to the bottom of what Jesus both said and meant. If you like to study history, and especially the history of theological thought, they make a fascinating read. Most readers will be familiar with the Nicene Creed, a product begun at the first council, in Nicaea (now in Turkey,) in 325CE.

I mention all of this to make clear that when we are planning and being ministers in worship and liturgy today, we are carrying not just the history of what Jesus said and did, but also what various church communities and councils, along with those variously labelled reformers, heretics and prophets, have told us those words and actions might, or should, or could, mean. Similarly different denominations and traditions each have their preferred understanding and definition of some common Christian words, as well as their own special "church words and phrases." While some of these may not be in common usage outside of seminaries or academic circles, they continue to impact how worship is planned, executed, and evaluated at every level. I want to briefly discuss five such examples, all from our common historical heritage of the first thousand years of Christianity, to make our journey easier to navigate.

COMMUNION

Central to Christian worship is the celebration of the Lord's Supper, something Jesus asked us to do in memory of him. All Christians agree that the food we choose stands as a sign and symbol of the living and risen Jesus among us. Many also believe, especially historically, that they go beyond that. We are not here to reopen that discussion. It is, however,

---

1. https://www.wordonfire.org/articles/fellows/the-eucharist-and-what-jesus-meant-by-is/

important to know something of the breadth of understanding and importance with which communion is held across our family of traditions.

At the historical end, we have a belief in what is called either transubstantiation (literally "change of substance,") or consubstantiation, (literally "two substances existing together.") For those not familiar with the words, it suffices to understand that those who believe that the bread and wine are changed into the Body and Blood of the Living Christ, also believe that this miracle is so significant that everything else during the worship should revolve around it. It is the "high point" of Christian worship. In the same way, when someone receives this "communion" they too experience a "change of substance" and are made one with the Living Christ. As St. Augustine of Hippo (354–430 CE) taught in an Easter Sermon (#272): "When you receive the Eucharist you become what you eat."

It is easy to understand that, for communities who hold tightly to either of these beliefs, (technically all Catholics and Orthodox, most Anglican/Episcopals, many Lutherans, and some others,) there is a very strong desire (a "tradition") to be as accurate and reverent as possible when preparing to celebrate such a service. This tends to put the person who is there as the presider of such an act of worship, especially the one saying the words of Jesus known as the "institution narrative," in a very special and important role. This leads to our next phrase.

IN PERSONA CHRISTI

This Latin phrase literally means, not surprisingly, "in the person of Christ." It is similar but not the same as when a teacher might be said to be *in loco parentis*, standing in for the person of a parent. While the teacher is not the parent, just standing in during their absence, the priest is considered to be one with Christ, who is believed to be really present.

Some would say that the community gathered in prayer as the Body of Christ, is also *in persona Christi*, and therefore an ordained clergy is not essential, or even needed. However, for those who are used to only having ordained clergy act as presiders and preachers, (individuals who have been called and often anointed by a bishop to that position,) it may seem a bridge too far to suggest they have anything in common with a lead actor in a play or a soloist with an orchestra. After all, this is not someone playing Jesus, but someone in a unique way able to act as Christ in the world, able effectively to give God's blessing and announce God's forgiveness. The theology says that when someone acts as "priest" it is God in Christ who is acting.

How does this happen? You might well ask. That takes us to our next term.

ONTOLOGICAL CHANGE

Ontology is the study of "being." Probably the most common "ontological change" many men experience is parenthood. While obviously a mother experiences an ontological change too, hers is significantly driven and paralleled by the physical changes to and in her body. She cannot ignore it, and it has a visible result, the child. When a man becomes a father there is no parallel change in his physicality. Psychology may suggest there may be changes in his mind and self-understanding, but these he can ignore. A mother has no such choice.

Similarly, when a person is ordained a minister or priest the Christian tradition held, and many still hold, that they undergo a change in their being, enabling them to be able to engage with the Living God in a special way. This change of being or status is what qualifies them to act *in persona Christi* and dispense God's blessings, forgiveness and sacraments.

But again, inquiring minds might ask, what if someone *thinks* they have been ordained but the bishop was a fraud? (It has happened!) or they *say* they have been ordained, but haven't? (That's happened too!) And there's always been the reality that humans, even saints, are not perfect or without fault. If the actions of an ordained person do not live up to the expected standards, can God still act through them in the world? Are, for example, their blessings and sacraments still valid? Centuries ago, the church had to come up with an answer for those situations.

EX OPERE OPERATO AND *EX OPERE OPERANTIS*

As any good student of Martin Luther will tell you, God is not limited by human competence or lack thereof. Grace is the freely available gift of God for which we need and can do nothing. Therefore, way back in the fourth century, the leaders of the Christian community coined the Latin phrase *ex opere operato*, which literally means, "by the work it is worked." That's why the church has, since then, had external ways of judging if a sacrament or blessing, or forgiveness has been given. Take, for example, baptism. All the Chrisian churches now agree that it doesn't matter if you are baptized by the Pope, your grandmother, or some itinerant preacher (even a fake one,) as long as the correct formulae is used, you are baptized. (The correct formulae being "(name,) I baptize you in the name of the Father, and of the Son and of the Holy Spirit, amen," while pouring water three times over the head of the person or immersing them under running water if that is available.) Any grace given is a direct gift from God to the person, irrespective of the minister in between. This, however, leads us to the other half of this Latin duo.

Ex opere operantis means "by the work of the worker." We, as recipients of God's grace, can't do anything to be worthy of it but we can refuse to accept the gift. The way this is usually expressed is that we must have a "right or good disposition." We have free will, so each of us can always say "no" to the Divine offer. As the old line goes: "It takes two to tango."

God is never limited by human failure, but also never over-rules our free will. These two Latin phrases work together to bring us to our final "church word."

METANOIA

Metanoia is a Greek word which is used in the scriptures to describe what happens when someone decides to change their ways and point their life in a new direction because of meeting Jesus and the power of the Holy Spirit. One could suggest Paul had a moment of metanoia on the road to Damascus, and that the close followers of Jesus had one at Pentecost, when they had gone into that room as fearful disciples but came out as fearless apostles.

Addicts often describe a moment when they "hit bottom" and decide to find a new direction for their life. This is a moment of metanoia. It is not about solving all the problems, but about facing and then trying to walk in a new direction, with a new intent.

These five words or phrases basically encompass the work and purpose of every Christian community, though it most certainly is not a straight, linear path. (I remember a high school art teacher continually reminding us that there are no straight lines in nature, a habit the Creator seems to continue to follow when dealing with us even today.)

The journey of "church" and "worship" is a dance between the individual, the community and the Divine, involving relationships, structures which, hopefully, guide the way to freedom, and ultimately both spiritual and personal growth, fruits of metanoia. The work of every minister is to teach and facilitate this dance and yet not get in the way; to prepare and enable the individual and community, to say "yes" to the grace of God coming into their life. We are the servants of those in the dance, Creator with created, Loving parent God with adopted daughters and sons. Our texts and scripts are our raw materials. How we use them is the topic of this book.

Prologue

IF YOU ALWAYS SAY the words "I love you" in the same way, you should probably never plan to become a performer, preacher, or liturgical planner or presider. While many unique factors help identify these different careers, this book explores the many ways in which the training and skill development of the liturgical planner, presider and preacher (viewed as distinct roles) can learn from the training and work-world of the live performing artist. It's all about communication, where we strive to make the words, notes, and steps flesh, taking them off the page and into peoples' lives.

In history we see that, no matter where the location, theater and religion always begin together. As communities developed around the globe, all religion was performed ritually, even theatrically; and all theater, at least to begin with, was about engaging the gods and spirits. Coming from this same apparently natural inclination and intuitive human place, these companion professions and their concomitant trainings have significant overlaps. A performer isn't a priest, except when they are. A priest isn't a performer, except when they are. And neither is a preacher, except . . . well, you get the idea.

To do their job, all three professionals need to learn a lot more than just memorizing the words or actions. Whether as performer, preacher, or presider, when we're doing the job three common and essential points are non-negotiable:

- The work and training are always rooted in both defining and refining our intention.
- The work is culturally expressed and passed on through spoken words (which, as we have said, also constitute musical notes and choreography).

- However, the majority of the communication (an amazing 60 to 90 percent) is not about the words themselves but having both a body and breath in time and space with which to deliver them.[1]

Throughout the book we will return frequently to these three essential topics of intentionality, the centrality of scripts, and having a body with breath in time and space.

While being a writer is somewhat different, one can always evaluate a new liturgical or performative script or production by whether or not the producer and planner has honored these three essentials of effective human communication.

Those who train performers clearly know this. They've spent decades, even centuries in some countries and cultures, perfecting methods of training and preparation, with specialist teams to help in all the component activities (movement, breathing, voice projection, posture, timing, etc.) and supporting crafts that are needed to bring the script to life.

INTENTION

While a good experience of liturgy and/or the performing arts might be described as "magical," none of them are a trick or illusion. They all create something real, using a mix of talent and work, as well as that something extra which is the spirit of the moment. Similarly, all three careers are not merely mental activities but whole-body ones. They all strive to engage the person and the spirit, to express the felt emotions and the logical thoughts, to be pragmatic as well as inspirational.

In both the performer's audience and liturgical congregation, we hope to experience that special moment when "something happens" and we're left moved and even changed. Yet, while actors, musicians and dancers train their physical skills extensively, most who preside and preach at church worship have little more than a few books and local examples on which to build such abilities. They'll usually have plenty of classroom learning about theology and scripture, about patristics and ethics, but the time allotted to standing in front of a congregation and working is, in most cases, dismally short and under-resourced. Imagine

---

1. These numbers for what percentage of face-to-face communication is non-verbal come from various sources and were summarized in an online article on the University of Texas Permian Basin's BA in Communications program. https://online.utpb.edu/about-us/articles/communication/how-much-of-communication-is-nonverbal/

the performance quality of a piece of theater, music, or dance if the artist had only been taught the *history* and *theory* of their art, not the *practice*. I doubt many audience members would return after the intermission!

While preachers and presiders could seek out great exponents of their craft and witness them live and in person, how many do? How many travel across a city, let alone a country, to experience and learn from a colleague who is gifted at creating that necessary liminal space which invites those present to be open to the potential grace of that unique moment? I suspect they're few and far between. Recent experience, since COVID, would suggest that even searching on YouTube or zoom is rare.

The cult of the individual is not appropriate for church, so we're not aiming for the ecclesiastical version of Oscar winners, despite the reputation of some TV or megachurch evangelists. However, we do need to ask what support and resources a liturgical planner, preacher and/or presider needs to continue improving at their craft of bringing people into a liminal proximity to, and dance with the Divine (who is always present) and inviting the Spirit to work on each as only God can. How do we create spaces where vulnerable and stressed people can feel safe enough to let down their guard and become open to a Spirit who has the scary reputation of transforming lives? The best place to start as a student is to work with people who can facilitate it happening to us personally so that we can experience what we are hoping to engender in others. Excellent mentors are few and far between, I fear.

This admittedly scary vulnerability to being willingly overwhelmed by the Divine requires us to let go and trust the power that moves us. Even for only a couple of hours in a dimly lit theater or concert hall, creating an environment in which people feel safe to let go of control is hard enough, let alone creating it for a lifetime of tomorrows. Yet I would suggest that if we've experienced, and indeed expect, this gift in the theater or a concert, then we have the right to expect such a thing in church too. Martin Luther was correct when he asked, "Must the devil have all the best tunes?" Like him, we hope the answer is a resounding "no."

In the arts this happens as an alchemy of skill and gift (which are not the same things), people working as a team over time to a common aim and purpose—in other words, a common intention. In church, one would think success might be easier to achieve, since the primary collaborator is the Divine. However, parish evaluations from the last forty or more years would suggest that most Christian liturgical congregations don't experience such alchemy on anything like the frequency one might hope or expect.[2]

WORDS (TEXTS AND SCRIPTS) . . .

The Christian invitation for this work comes most pointedly from the opening of John's Gospel: "In the beginning was the Word, and the Word was with God. And the Word was God . . . The word was made flesh and lived among us." (Jn.1:1,14)

The work of performers, preachers, and presiders is to take the texts or scripts they're given or, for example, in the case of preachers, create for themselves, and make them flesh for an audience or congregation. It's the way we ensure that what we say is *communicated*, which in turn means that *the meaning* the performer, preacher, or presider intends is delivered as accurately and fully as possible to those interested in listening. We'll explore the implications of this essential step in Chapter 5.

Crucial to note here is that words (even ones we hold sacred) cannot be used without being interpreted. Saying that all written words need to be interpreted when they are spoken aloud can be a difficult subject for some, suggesting that scripture and prayers might have multiple meanings. It might be helpful to think of a musical score, and how it sounds different if an enthusiastic beginner is playing it or a concert-level musician. As we will explore in future chapters, performers are not just presenting what is on the page, but what lies inside what is on the page, including the silence and sub-text. The words are ultimately only symbols of meaning and understanding, based on a commonly held (though rarely universal) agreement of both definition (which often changes over time) and cultural meaning (which can vary even more freely).

As the wise scripture professor's adage goes: "A text quoted out of context is always a pretext for something else." Therefore, we cannot explore how we interpret words without also exploring our intention, along with our understanding of what we want to communicate when we use those words in that way, at that time, with that vocal inflection, and that eye contact (or not), in that social or private context. Phew! If any one of these variables isn't in alignment with what we're trying to say, the words

---

[2]. The research published by BARNA in 2021, based on their The State of Your Church 2020 project, suggests that 38% of practicing Christians and 50% of what they define as "Churched Adults" leave their Sunday services "Disappointed" always, most of the time, or half the time." See https://www.barna.com/research/churchgoers-feel/

can mean something very different from what we intended. However, if we stopped every single time before speaking to consider all the possible variations of parameters and how they might be interpreted, we would say an awful lot less. (Possibly a good thing!) Our conversations (and certainly our communications by text) would be a lot more stilted, with overthinking reducing the flow of communication. This is why any professional communicator prepares a text, edits it numerous times, then rehearses it repeatedly. We practice in advance and then, on the day, we keep an internal ear attuned to what we're saying and *how* we're saying it, as in a constant feedback loop.

Human communication may be delightfully amusing and heartfelt when left to beginners and amateurs (social media is full of such "memes"). But if we're asking people to pay to listen to us, whether that be by buying tickets or putting money in the collection plate, we need to have a handle on our craft—it's professional courtesy.

. . . MADE FLESH

Using the opening verses from the Gospel of John mentioned above seems the most appropriate place to base this work. The Good News is designed to work when it is made flesh. Some of my best experiences of "church" have been in a theater or concert hall, and if I ever need a quick "fix" of "Good News," I just find the Broadway production of *Kinky Boots—The Musical* on YouTube.

You hopefully have such go-to experiences yourself, maybe specific pieces of music, novels or poetry, or movies. We do well to remember that whatever the Divine essence of life is, it most certainly isn't limited to the confines of the church walls or other places of worship, or even to a sacred text written thousands of years ago. The Word and the Good News is a *living* presence and never fully contained or limited. We forget this at our peril. Whether it's a religious text or secular, papyrus or eBook, Shakespeare or blogger, if we're going to undertake to be the contemporary interpreters of any of it "in the flesh," we must do our due diligence and train appropriately.

HAVING A BODY WITH BREATH IN TIME AND SPACE

This book was written as a reflective and practical journey for liturgical planners, presiders and preachers (whether experienced professionals or folks just starting out), with the intention of helping us all grow in our ability to keep the words fresh and in the moment, even if we're saying them for the eighth time this week and have been doing so for many months or years.

Another way to think about this invitation is to approach each text every time as if the ink were still wet, as if we were the first person ever to see and then say these words in public. Imagine, if you like, being in the community in ancient Corinth or Phillipi when a letter arrived from Paul or another of the church leaders in Jerusalem. The invitation is to experience the words and intention for the first time, fresh, with the body and breath we have today, at a particular point in time and history. This is the approach an actor takes every time they step onto the stage. Every night is, in some ways, opening night, and the ink on every script is always still wet.

The outline for this book is loosely based on that of an extended preparation period for a theatrical production. As listed in the chapter headings, we start with the issue of casting (and miscasting), then move through script preparation, meeting the crew, rehearsals, background work, and then openings and closings. At the end of each chapter is a set of questions on which readers can reflect.

Much of this book is based on my own experience of being bi-cultural, with one foot in the performing arts and the other in liturgy and church life. On the one hand, I've trained and worked in drama and theater for over fifty years, as well as being a musician and dancer for some of that time. I started working with parish ministry in my teens and have never stopped. In terms of limitations, I write as an older white male from the UK who has lived the second half my life on the west coast of America. I grew up in the post-Second World War Roman Catholic world in England, which was a different culture than contemporary Catholicism elsewhere. I've had the chance to work across cultural and religious boundaries as a high school teacher, retreat giver, parish minister, and hospice chaplain, celebrating the action of the Holy Spirit in each place.

I have made the choice to, wherever possible, use non-gendered pronouns, choosing "they" and "them" in place of needing to continually write "her or his or theirs," etc. Quotations, of course, will be given as they were written.

Through this journey some truths I've learned are self-evident, and I invite everyone to remember this simple one: As long as we show up with a *body* and *breath*, with the *intention* to be truthful and loving, the Word can speak, be it in church, on a drama stage, in a concert hall, or during a dance work. But without our turning up in this way, with the intention to use all the skills at our disposal to communicate the author, or Author, nothing will be truly heard. This, I believe, is our covenantal relationship with our vocation: To get better at turning up, with a set of advanced skills and experience, so that the Spirit can do Divine work. As the practical mystic St. Teresa of Avila (1515–1582) said many centuries ago, "Christ has no other body now but yours:"

> *Christ has no body but yours,*
> *No hands, no feet on earth but yours,*
> *Yours are the eyes with which he looks*
> *Compassion on this world,*
> *Yours are the feet with which he walks to do good,*
> *Yours are the hands, with which he blesses all the world.*
> *Yours are the hands, yours are the feet,*
> *Yours are the eyes, you are his body.*

1

Getting Cast
Or Is It Miscast??

Without a voice the script will never be heard. Without the right voice the script will never be understood.

FOR TOO LONG LITURGICAL training in many churches has "put the cart before the horse," texts before skilled proclamation, effectively prioritizing books and rules over living people and experience.

In the view of liturgical ministry we'll be exploring, the minister (ordained or lay, paid or volunteer,) is still the "horse" doing the work. The "cart," containing all the paraphernalia that has accumulated over 1,700 years, is their wonderful, shared resource, but should not be a rule book. The cart is full of many great assets and treasures, able to be powerful, enduring symbols of, and ways to engage with, God's love and mercy. It also contains some outdated and "no longer fit for use" baggage. However, ultimately the leader and the community do the work of liturgy or worship, of incarnating and reflecting the Divine presence in the world, not the contents of the cart. For this understanding of their role, leaders need training that is based, like that of an actor, on practical skills, and an understanding of how those skills manifest with the leader's unique humanity.

This approach has received a lot of less than positive attention over the centuries, necessitating the development of concepts such as "*ex opere operato*" regarding the ordained minister, as well as "*ex opere operantis*" regarding a congregation as mentioned in the Introduction. We will set aside any fears about judging "worthiness" and look simply towards skills training. We are no longer gathering for ritual to appease an angry and vengeful god or gods but to renew and celebrate our love-based relationship with a Creator who wants nothing more than to walk in the cool of the evening with their Creation (Gen 3:8).

If we are looking to do the work of "making the Word flesh" we must understand where the liturgical community of "church" has come to, and why it is in a time of transition. We'll pick up the extensive journey of centuries just sixty years ago.

The Second Vatican Council (1962–1965) was not only a watershed moment for the Roman Church, but its ripples were felt across much of the Christian world. We reference them therefore not just for what they had to say about Roman Catholic theology, liturgy and life, but also for what they were able to contribute to other denominations. In this regard, Vatican II's document *Lumen Gentium* ("The Light of the World") importantly articulates five ways in which the living Christ is present in the world and these ways all depend on people with bodies and breath, and none on things or books. Our Reformed sisters and brothers, among others, saw this as a significant step in the right direction of putting the "horse" back in front of the "cart."

- In the celebration of the Lord's Supper, where Christ is present as the gathered community and minister, and in the bread and wine.
- In the other sacraments, where Christ is present such that when someone baptizes or confirms, it is Christ who acts.
- In God's word, when the scriptures are proclaimed for the community, for it is Christ who speaks as the Word of God made flesh.
- When the church prays and sings, for Christ has promised "Where two or three are gathered in my name, I am there in their midst."
- In the church itself, which is Christ's body, with Christ as the head. The liturgy is an exercise of Christ's priestly office, carried out by those baptized in the name of the Trinity.

One of the revolutionary truths which was revealed by this list, as if for the first time for some, was the fact that all five ways individually represent a total and full opportunity to engage with the risen and living Christ of the Gospels. They are not in a ranked order, but each instance is the opportunity for a complete Divine engagement. God and the Christ is either present or not, neither more nor less. God does not come in fractions or percentages.

Therefore, when we are looking to cast others, or be cast ourselves in this role of being part of the presence of the living Christ in the world, (*in persona Christi*,) we must be ready to step outside our personal story and history, and into something much bigger, our calling to be disciples.

What we are exploring by reflecting on "casting" is whether, just as we have to do with performers, someone genuinely has the charism or calling for the work of liturgy as well as the skills. To misquote the Jesus of scripture (Matt 22:14), "Many may feel called but few are qualified to be cast in a lead role." And if they are cast, do they have enough raw talent as well as the right training to sustain the job? One suspects we have all been to enough concerts and shows to know that enthusiasm and commitment are great, but not always enough. St. Paul tried to explain this to us when he wrote that there is a wide range of gifts needed to make the Body of Christ whole and work, but each must be in the correct place (Eph 4:11–13, 1 Cor 12:12–27). Too many church leaders throughout history have tended to assume that ordination is sufficient, and that the gifts will come later. Would that this were true! Some gifts do indeed come with experience, but find it hard to build on inadequately prepared foundations.

The gifts needed by good, let alone great, communicators and community leaders are in many ways instinctual things, not shown by the results of a test or exam. We're talking about someone's ability to share, to communicate their own humanness as well as God's transforming love. Sharing is a huge risk and takes an enormous amount of generosity. (There can also be, as history has proven, a sizable amount of ego involved too!) These skills might be able to be taught but some talent, some seed, and a great desire to learn needs to be discerned first. A place exists for all the gifts of God in the whole Body, but behind an altar or lectern, or in the pulpit might not be the right or best one for many, including some who currently have that role. It is a special level of leadership failure, and potentially abuse, when, as St. Paul might have said, "The ear is used as a mouth and the heart is used as a hammer."

CASTING FOR THE JOB

For the actor, getting cast is usually a great high, whether as a professional ("I can eat again!") or an amateur ("They really liked me! Or maybe they were just desperate . . . but they seemed to like me too!")

While an amateur and professional might differ in the extent of their training, all good actors (whether paid or not) bring an active curiosity for exploring the humanness of their character, their strengths and weaknesses, constraints and openness, gifts and prejudices. The actor knows, even before they read the script, that the real play will be explored within those conflicts and parameters, within what we call the sub-text. If they're not able to unpack these realities, including the personal failings experienced through the rehearsal period, the play won't reach its potential. Not every character will have a dramatic or redemptive arc through the script, but the job is to explore whatever is there for your character within the overall arc of the production.

Everyone brings an idea of themselves as being human (or, in some cases, a fantasy of being superhuman!) to the job table, aware of their gifts and talents, their degrees and such, or the lack of them. In theater it's regarded as a plus when an actor also brings the vulnerability and possibility of what is still to come, of potential for growth and for finding hidden depths. That is just as exciting to a good director as all the known talents and trained gifts which are listed on the actor's resume. A good director will have an intuition for those too. In most job interviews the boss wants to know what's on offer and your reliability, not your openness to finding yourself in the process of "losing yourself" in your work. A theater director is rarely looking for someone who says, "I know all about this character and I've played the part many times before. I have it down!"

What they're looking for is an appreciation for the complexity and the humor, a unique perspective, or the potential surprises of the character, as well as why playing the role this time is different from playing it five years ago. They're hoping for a sense of excitement in an actor taking the journey to find more. They're also looking for someone who's okay with searching and failing (with the rest of the cast) in the public forum which is the rehearsal room, until possible—and ideally better—answers are found communally. A good actor/director relationship is an explorative mentorship through the potential of the script and the characters. A good director knows that the actors will not just be playing the text, but will be inhabiting the sub-text, where the spirit of the piece, the drives and motivations behind the words, lives and breathes. In other words, a director must believe an actor can embody the intent of the piece.

At theatrical auditions hearing a director say something along the lines of, "I could work with them," or "I think they would work well with each other" is not unusual. We say this because we're looking for the possibility of communal discovery and revelation. While church folks are keen to quote the Book of Revelation 21:5 ("and behold, I am making all things new"), it is often folks like actors, with their directors and team, who are committed to trying to make the words come alive in a revelation "before our very eyes" as if the ink were still wet. By contrast, in my experience and by popular lore, "making anything new" (as in "doing it a different way than before") is rarely welcome in churches.

And then there's this other truth: It can be very sad when a talented actor isn't chosen for a part because, in the eyes of the director, they're just not right for this production. That doesn't mean that an actor could never take that role, but in the vision of a particular director, the whole production, this time, cannot be made complete with what they feel are the wrong parts. (Once I heard a director offer solace by saying: "You're great, an absolute Cadillac of a performer, but we're building a Toyota, and the parts need to match.") Maybe someone has a distinctive charisma on stage, which throws off the balance of the cast. Maybe it's about someone lacking the skill of controlling or directing their personality.

This is about intuition, alchemy, synergy, and probably sometimes an unfortunate dose of personal preference and even prejudice too. But that's why directors get paid the big bucks (even in amateur theater, where often no one else is paid), because they're the ones leading the team to bring it all together, delivering both the text and the sub-text, the words and the meaning behind the words.

Not to be cast when you feel confident you're the best person for a role, or not get a role you've wanted to create for many years, is very hard. And often there aren't objective factors in which to find solace. It just wasn't your turn.

For the successful cast member, this all means that you were chosen over a person some may have thought was more gifted or capable because the director felt you were a better overall fit for the cast and the production. They saw something in you which was more interesting and hopeful than what the other actors already had in their shop window. Congratulations!

Sometimes, especially in community theater companies, a female actor might get a role because the script calls for four men and only three guys auditioned. In these situations, it's up to the director and producer to ask some important questions. Can a certain role be played by a woman rather than a man? And if so, should she do it as a woman, and change all the pronouns etc., in the script, or in "drag," because the role must be male? Will a more talented female actor in a supporting role take the focus away from a less-talented male actor in the lead? (In my experience it's rarely the other way around.)

In the theater the answer, it is said, "is always in the script," and a lot of scripts are available from which to choose, so we also have the choice to let go of one and choose another. That's not always an option in a church community.

CASTING THE PREACHER

Of all the liturgical ministers, the preacher absolutely has the hardest job.

They have no provided scripts, but lots of expectations and challenges. If this were a play, the preacher would be both the author as well as the narrator, the cast member called on to "break the fourth wall" which usually stays intact during a play.[1] In theater language the preacher is tasked with identifying both with the action of the piece as well as with the audience, a "go between."

From the perspective of the performing arts, the preacher as author has most in common with the company of writers, which is a whole other skill set outside the scope of this book. However, as performers they must also be like improvisation artists and even stand-up comedians, as well as classical or jazz musicians called to play or sing both the notes written as well as create variations and cadenzas that fit within the flow of the whole piece. This all takes real natural talent as well as good training and lots of practice.

---

1. The "fourth wall" in a theater is where the curtain or proscenium arch is or would be. The other three walls are the stage and set, but the fourth wall is transparent, existing in everyone's minds but not in reality. The actors are rarely called upon to "break the fourth wall" by addressing the audience because the actors aren't talking and moving as if they were "here, now." They are "somewhere else, and not now." While this is one of the ways in which liturgy is not nor meant to be a piece of theater, our buildings do tend to create a "fourth wall" at the altar rail or the historic rood screen, which separates the contemporary Holy of Holies from the ordinary people. It's important to notice that this architectural feature can have a significant effect on the way people respond in the space.

As a preacher you might be one in a series or a vacation "pulpit-filler." This might be for a very special occasion, like a keynote address but in a service, or a life transition, such as a graduation, wedding, or funeral. Or, of course, it might just be your turn on a rotation of people (sometimes a rotation of one) who gets to preach each time the community gathers. You should always remember that you can say "no, thank you," but if you say "yes," then the work begins.

In all these situations, but especially in that last one—where you are "it" on a rotation of one, and you must preach every week or even every day—it can feel more like a heavy imposition rather than a delightful, life/career-affirming invitation. But some good news exists even here, for we can choose to view and experience this not as a "monotony of being chosen *again*" but as an invitation to go deeper into our craft, ourselves, and our communal story with the Author who calls and casts us in life. This journey is, unfortunately, usually not undertaken without self-revelation and risk, which is the world of the good actor. Saying "I have nothing to say today" takes immense courage, but one can also use the skills of "improv" and create a dialogue with the congregation on what they see in the readings and the work of God and/or the church in the world. This approach has risks too, of course.

It's important to remember that no matter if this is your first sermon or your thousandth, whether you bring a lifetime of experience and training to this invitation or the innocence and naivete of youth, if you do your research, prepare with prayer, strive to speak the Spirit's truth, and yet make the message your own, it will work. Whether you were picked from a list of "headliners" or from a pool of just one, you were chosen. You are the one with a body and breath, here and now. Without you the contemporary word won't even be spoken, let alone become flesh.

If the humility of the moment can call from you something to rival the eloquence of your greatest heroes and heroines, then rejoice. If the mundaneness of the moment seems to bring you nothing, seek the ground within the readings (script) you are given or choose, and root yourself there, with the "wet ink" of the moment. Seeing even a small shoot rise from such earth brings much joy on a quiet day. After all, very few people ever said, "that sermon was too short!"

Like it or not, you were picked, and as a professional you're expected to deliver the goods. Often an isolated activity with no group rehearsal, accepting this casting requires an internal discipline to the work and having a good sense of the wider support and resources you have available.

Most importantly, like an actor understanding the play's author, you must be secure in your relationship with the divine source of your inspiration, trusting you can show up (with, as we have said, an available body and breath, with intellect and intention), and then get out of the way for what needs to be enfleshed. The questions which often work for me in this situation are, "What do I need to hear someone say about these readings? Where's the challenge for me? Where's the humor? (The Spirit is often a jokester, and the joke is usually on us!) Most importantly, where's the Good News?"

CASTING THE PRESIDER

Casting presiders is very denominationally dependent. For churches where clergy are appointed it's basically the luck of the draw. No generally accepted standards exist for any of the practical parts of ministerial training or learned competence in communication skills. Nor does any post-ordination remedial help exist for those challenged in these areas by natural introversion, shyness, or a lifetime of bad habits or examples. Of course, plenty of faith and faith development can be had, along with goodwill and theological rigor in celebrating the sacraments, which most dioceses seem to feel is sufficient. Parishioners may think differently[2].

Talking to a seminary group once, I asked the question, "Do you see yourself becoming a minister of the church or a minister of the gospel?" Some in the group appreciated the distinction, others didn't. If I were to simplify the different responses, some saw their function as just that, functionaries of the sacramental system which the church holds, guards, and maintains. Their position seemed to be that this is all that's needed for eternal life, which is effectively the only purpose of the earthly experience. They tended to have a more legalistic approach to theology. Those who saw themselves more as becoming ministers, one might say servants, of the gospel saw their priesthood as about facilitating a relationship between the faithful and the Divine, particularly with Jesus as the incarnate one, a journey with which they also needed to engage personally in an ever-deeper way. Their theology was more compassionate and relational.

---

2. Go to the website of any theological school in the English-speaking world and count the number of professors for worship or liturgy as compared to scripture or systematic and moral theology. Some have none. Some have just one Adjunct Lecturer. Preaching does fare better, it's true, but not much. Ministers are frequently trained as an academic exercise, not a practical one.

To use theater language: The first group was confident in the immutability of the inbuilt efficacy of the text provided by their church. (*Ex opere operato.*) The second group was aware that the important part was the sub-text which exists within the text. Helping people explore that sub-text for themselves was the freedom of the children of God of which Jesus spoke. (*Ex opere operantis.*)

For the first group church services and the Sacraments are the essential path, often with communion as the highpoint, source and fountain of all the divine grace available in this life.

For the second group, however, if I were to put my words into their mouths, I would suggest that the Sacraments are the "wonderfully guaranteed minimum" of God's ongoing, grace-filled interaction with God's people. These moments function as the scaffolding of our spiritual lives, but never limit the flow of God's response, creativity, or spontaneity.

This is one way of articulating the fundamentally different approach to the sacramental history of Christianity which various groups have made, especially since the Reformation. I believe this understanding is particularly pertinent for the work of evangelism in the twenty-first century. If the Word of God as a living encounter with the Risen Christ cannot be allowed to risk being made creative and generative flesh, then worship will risk being seen as a set of archaic rituals, with overtones, once again, of magical incantations.

The issue becomes increasingly significant as more and more parishes in the cultural West have clergy appointed who originate in the cultural South and East. While the love, faith, and commitment of those appointed aren't in doubt, a mutual lack of familiarity with both a different culture and language, and often spirituality, is an extra challenge which deserves vastly better support and standards. The same is true for anyone who has English or American as a first culture and language being asked to serve communities which don't.

In theater terms we're talking about different understandings of the sub-text within a liturgical text as well as different cultural practices in which the text is "made flesh." While dioceses who appoint their clergy are very familiar with this reality, a limited (by prejudice or practicality,) casting pool makes alternatives difficult to find.

While the perception is true that clear communication between clergy and people is a good thing and to be encouraged, it is frequently not considered essential. All that seems to matter is that the clergy faithfully and with good intent follow the rubrics and words of the prayer books, as in "say the black, do the red." In this approach the faithful should accept and support this service in obedience to the rites of the church and the local bishop, taking from it whatever they can, remaining open to the Divine's offer of grace contained in the celebration of the sacraments. This is not far removed from the medieval "cart before the horse" approach mentioned earlier.

Any extra gifts or talents a pastor might have, beyond the common ritual expectations of the diocese, are a bonus and rarely seem to come into the decision-making process for casting, regardless of the community's need. This minimalistic approach is useful in these days of (supposed) ministry shortages, but for now we'll simply comment that it seems less than optimal, especially in an era of prioritizing evangelization and outreach. This is neither efficient nor effective. Some dioceses have been exploring the placement of trained lay ecclesial ministers in parishes and then offer what are known as "supply priests" or "pulpit supply" for the sacramental necessities. Hope for the future can be evident in this action, but so may be the prejudice that excludes some otherwise capable participants from the lead casting pool.

For faith communities that can advertise a position, interview various candidates, and eventually call a new pastor or staff member, the role of the "casting director" is frequently taken on by a committee, often after a significantly lengthy internal process. That process will often have included a review of current demographics as well as recent "casting." In the Episcopal Church, for example, this document is known as the Parish Profile. Similarly, like an actor being able to read the script before auditioning, a potential new pastor can read such a Profile, as well as the mission statement and objectives of a community, and maybe even talk with the outgoing role holder.

While this process seems to have a lot to recommend it, it by no means guarantees perfectly matched results. In a sense, it's like the difference between an arranged marriage and a love-match. The result is revealed in the living out of the relationship and covenant. The job description may seem clear but, if you ask any pastor, the reality (sub-text) of this living agreement can never be completely expressed on a printed page (the text). A lot more is expected than just doing the job that was advertised, including the manner in which it is done.

I think the only other group of people who have anything like the job description of some of the solo full-time pastors I've known are single parents with four kids under 12, an aging parent, a dog, and of course a full-time job. All it took some years ago when they were young and everything felt possible (and hopefully they were in love), was a simple spoken "I do," but ten, twenty, thirty years later, the list of "oh, this is part of the job too" continues to be growing, like Mickey Mouse's nightmare in *Fantasia* with the water, buckets, and brooms. Way too many pastors are miscast in this or a very similar nightmare. The amazing grace and blessing is how many of these folks do indeed keep on showing up and doing the work to the best of their ability.

SOME CLOSING REFLECTIONS ON BEING CAST OR MISCAST

In my experience, theater groups and companies are generally a supportive environment for actors and theater folk. Firstly, that's because it's a rather iterant lifestyle where one needs to work with others to make the beauty happen, often in a relatively short window of time and with a small budget. The good news is that plenty of creative and important decisions can be made.

Liturgical leaders and worship communities often work with what feels like a very fixed situation or, at best, one offering only limited opportunities for creativity and variety, which can be rather stifling. This sense of limitation can just as easily come from the congregation as from the leadership, either locally or national. "Church" is often plagued by the frequently spoken (or even enshrined) mantra of "this is the way we do things here," which sets a sense of tradition firmly ahead of being "in the moment."

Tradition is not in and of itself a bad thing; indeed, we need it in order to build a ritual community. We cannot be reinventing everything every day or communicating without a common sense of grounding and meaning. (Cue here the great song from *Fiddler on the Roof*: Tradition![3]) However, tradition, as both Tevye and Golde discovered, may be a great place to start, but it cannot be the only place to stay. Our God is not the God of the past, or indeed of the future, but of the now, as in the popular works of Eckhart Tolle and Marilynne Robinson; or, if you prefer, the spiritual presentation of the likes of Jean-Pierre de Caussade or Ignatius of Loyola.

---

3. For an excellent exploration of this word and the issue the movie faced, as we will many times in this book, see the thirty minute piece "Why Findler on the roof is misunderstood". https://www.youtube.com/watch?v=63VTb_IWiqE.

I think part of the difference between theater and church in their work environments is due to the "embodied" nature of theater folks. Even though many actors feel themselves to be introverts (yes, truly), we stretch, scream, sweat, and generally suffer with each other during rehearsals, and then go for a drink afterwards. Clergy tend to be more isolated and possibly more cerebral. Some drinking occurs (especially with the Catholics, Episcopalians, and Lutherans, some of whom offer "Theology on Tap" events at their parishes), but I've never heard a group of them going off for a karaoke night or to other therapeutic outlets.

Of course, introverts and extroverts are just two ways of being along a whole continuum, with performers, presiders, and preachers over its entire length. However, the work for all of us is to "make the word(s) flesh," not to "make the script into a concrete idea or intellectual construct." The topic of this book is, at root, about training in communication, so recognizing that, especially for Christian worship leaders, the Divine's invitation and call is not primarily linguistic is important. Just as actors aren't trying to be William Shakespeare or Anton Chekhov, for Christians the "Word" has already been spoken in history. Our job is to mirror and model ourselves after the one who we recognize as "the Word made flesh" and incarnate the message to the best of our ability to "speak" it today.

Within this imbalance are two very important four-letter words and how they interact and need each other: work and play.

Here is not the place to go into an extensive reiteration of the German Reformed theologian Jurgen Moltman's "The Theology of Play" and others' seminal and revelatory work on the subject. They are easily available through your favorite internet or AI platform. Maybe just a quote or two will help:

> *God creates playing. And man should play if he is to live as humanly as possible and to know reality, since it is created by God's playfulness.*[4]

> *In play we emulate God's actions who did not create the universe because it was a necessity. God is playful. He enjoys creating and playing.*[5]

---

4. https://www.christianitytoday.com/ct/2017/july-august/thou-shalt-have-good-time.html.

5. https://www.emotionallyhealthy.org/a-theology-of-play/.

When Jesus shocked the disciples by saying that unless they learnt how to become like little children they wouldn't find the entryway to heaven (Mt.18:3), he was inviting us all, among other things, to play with him.

The invitation to be cast in a play, which will mean undertaking a lot of work, is an invitation to join the creator (Divine or otherwise) in the joyous exploration of co-creating beauty and newness and even revelation. The invitation is not about getting it right, for there's rarely just one "right" way to do or say anything; it's about taking the risk to be alive and explore what might work best in a specific time, place, and community.

The same is true for the invitation to lead (as presider) a community on the journey to engage with the Divine Other, or (as preacher) to try and unpack the meaning of the creative playful work of that Divine Other as manifested at this time. Play without work is self-indulgence (limited in possibility, though not necessarily a bad thing, as any four-year old will attest), and work without play is, if not slavery, at least indentured servitude. Yet across much of the educational world, play is under threat. Recess is being reclaimed for test revisions, and playtime must now be more productive, with sports leagues and potential extra-curricular resume listings. This "war on play" didn't happen overnight, but it seems to getting worse.[6]

An important part of the rehearsal process is to "play" with the words and relationships within a production. Another is exploring the sub-text of a piece by looking at it from different perspectives, each of which offers a unique view and voice. "Play" is, if you like, working to find the best way to say "I love you" in this new moment and place.

Being cast in a play invites us to explore, with a child-like imagination, fearlessness and creativity, everything which might be contained within and behind the text. This is the work, the invitation, each time someone breaks open the Word or leads the community in prayer.

This is God's invitation: do you want to come out and play?

QUESTIONS FOR REFLECTION

1. Make a list of all the roles you are currently playing in this open-ended run called "My Life in This Parish." If you've ever been given

---

6. Psychology Today has offered several articles on the value of play for logic and other life skills. See, for example, https://www.psychologytoday.com/us/blog/your-brain-at-work/202208/unlocking-the-cognitive-benefits-of-play.

a job description, now might be a good time to re-read it for a laugh, or maybe a cry. (Your favorite beverage might be helpful here too.)

2. Which of these roles are sufficiently important to you and the community that you want to make the time and create the space to explore new growth in these areas? If that means dropping some roles from your current repertoire, at least for a while, how do you and the parish feel about that?

3. If "Liturgical Leader" and/or "Preacher" are anywhere near the top of your list, would you like to prioritize these roles? That would need a commitment to turn up for "rehearsals and cast meetings" so that you can discover how this casting looks on your shoulders at this point in your life with this community.

4. If you're in a well-funded and resourced parish, with a leadership team, regular vacations, and sabbaticals, along with ongoing formation and training, I invite you to (a) say a daily prayer of gratitude and (b) think about how you might be able to help other liturgical leaders in your area who are much less well-supported. If you can do it across denominational lines, it's better still.

2

Meeting the Director and Production Team, and Beginning to Explore the Script

Words and ideas do not exist in a vacuum; they live in a world imagined by someone. Who that someone is always matters.

ONCE ONE HAS BEEN cast in a creative piece, the next step is usually receiving the script and finding out when the "table read" is going to be. This is the name for the first time the performers will meet the rest of the cast, the stage manager, the director, and any other production team members able to be there (lighting, costumes, choreographer, etc.), often literally all sitting around a table or in a circle. It is usually an exciting moment. Often a scale model of the set will be available so you can see where doors, steps, hidden exits, etc., are. After some words of welcome, an explanation of what the production is going to feel and look like, you all just read the script as your characters, from beginning to end, with the stage manager adding in any stage descriptions or other notes which are included in the script.

While any actors and other performers reading this will probably be, "Yes, fine, moving on . . ." I'd like to give a moment for our worship colleagues to soak it all in and get over their envy. Performers get to play in a room full of other creative people, and it can really be fun, if also a little intimidating. Too often being a preacher or presider is a solitary occupation, devoid of fun and collective creativity. This is a great shame, because playing together is where we really learn so much important "stuff" about being human in community. It would be interesting to do a study of the play life of ministers as children. Did they have siblings or other playmates? Was this a skill they never got to explore or learn? When did we as adults stop playing as a way of engaging the transcendent?

The first thing for presiders who are preparing to lead a liturgy to notice, (in other words, in the role of the "lead actor" as well as maybe the "director" if they are the planner too,) is that a model exists here to help us remember we're part of a team. The more we're willing to engage with the team, the more support we should be able to feel as well as offer. Conversely, the more we act like a prima donna, projecting the idea that somehow we know more than everyone else, (even when, technically, we probably do) and generally set ourselves apart, the less support we'll feel.

In a church situation, that same person who is "the lead" will also often be the equivalent to the director. The theater model helps us to remember they are different functions needing different skills. A theater company will often also have an artistic director, who has the long-term vision of the company in their care. They probably chose the script the company is working on and possibly the director for this specific production. In some churches one could think of the artistic director as the diocesan moderator or bishop, or maybe the dean of a cathedral. In other situations, it could be the same person (the pastor) as the other two roles of production director and lead actor. This "artistic director" role is very important, especially when we're imagining how we might approach the relatedness of our major feasts/events (such as The Easter Triduum, Christmas, Pentecost, etc.), as well as looking at sequences such as the Advent Season, Lent, and then the long summer season, when things may slow down but still must be planned.

At this point, therefore, let us say a few words about the two directors involved, both for the overall company (artistic director) and a specific production.

THE DIRECTOR(S): INFLUENCES, RESPONSIBILITIES, AND EVALUATION

When someone is invited either to become the artistic director for a company or direct a specific production, the company's board will usually want to review any prior work and talk about the influences and vision the prospective candidate brings to the table. Have they worked with specific authors before? With which other companies have they worked? How did they treat the actors? Were they respectful of time and budget? Would they work with that group again? One would also want to check that a director was sensitive to a company's culture, social demographic, and overall purpose.

A prospective director should be able to talk about and justify their vision for a piece or a season. This might include how simple or complex a production they have in mind. (Remember, authors such as Shakespeare used virtually no sets and frequently used their own clothes regardless of whether the piece was set in ancient Rome or a fantasy island, yet Shakespearean plays can be done with elaborate staging and costumes too.) Similarly, in which time period or geographical placement would it be set? (For example, moving a play from one time and/or country to another, or one political situation to another, can help a piece have a new interpretation and a more powerful resonance for a contemporary audience.) Would they see changing any of the casting, for example to reflect the local community? (An all-white, male-dominated traditional cast of a play might not be well attended or accessed in a more culturally diverse and inclusive community. On the other hand, change simply for the sake of change rarely works well.) Gender roles can be very important to review too, particularly when regarding available talent, especially with amateur companies where, as mentioned above, talented women tend to outnumber available men by two or even five (or more!) to one.

A theater director should be honest about their skill set and potential weaknesses, for example, if they don't know much about lighting, or staging fights or choreography if needed. Finally, they should be able to show that they can lead a team, working well with others both on stage and behind the scenes. Success is not just about the final product ("did they do well?") but also the process ("would you invite them back?").

We can see the "artistic director" of a parish as the pastor, diocesan bishop or moderator, or even a national or international individual or committee. The more removed they are from the specific place where a liturgy will happen, the more their rules or guidelines will need to be enculturated. However, if artistic direction is in the hands of someone who is only interested in "direction" and not the "artistic" part, then that can seriously hinder the creative energy flow throughout the system. To paraphrase the Book of Proverbs: "Happy the community whose leader knows their own limitations."

THE SCRIPT

In a church setting the equivalent of the theater director is most commonly the pastor or another clergy person on the parish staff. However, the equivalent is possibly a liturgy or worship director or team who may be paid or volunteer. Whoever it is, when it comes to addressing the script a couple of significant additional parameters should be noted.

The first parameter is that word we've already begun to unpack, tradition. Cultural traditions held sway in theater for many centuries, and still do predominantly in some areas we've mentioned, such as Japanese Kabuki theater. However, church work can have the added weight of the tradition being thought to be divinely ordained; or, even if it's not formally recognized as that, for everyone to act as if it were. Most common, of course, are limitations on the role of women in some faith traditions, closely followed by what is regarded as acceptable for vesture or other clothing, physical room layout, décor, and music.

The second parameter we need to recognize is permission.

With a theater script which isn't yet in the public domain (which varies by country but is generally applied to works around a hundred years old), a company must purchase the rights to perform a script for a specific set of days, in a specific space/address which has a specific number of seats. By so doing, the company agrees to stipulations about what may or (more usually) may *not* be changed without specific permission. Rules can even extend to the relative size of the lettering for the author's name on the posters. If a work is no longer under copyright protection you can do whatever you like, because no one has legal standing (the heirs, estate, etc.) to sue you. Chekov or Ibsen may be turning in their graves, but we'll never know!

Within different faith communities there is a similarly wide range of attitudes: some operate as if everything is still under copyright, even though the actual script is 400 years old or older. Some churches release all copyrights so that permission to "make it work in your own time and space" is granted with access to the script, which might even be free to copy from the internet. The reason commonly used for a community needing this permission is for "inculturation," to make the texts work in a specific cultural context. While this is frequently used to mean non-white, non-male-dominated cultures, the reality is that there can be a wide range of cultural differences even within those communities, for example, between areas where agriculture is the main occupation as opposed to office work or manufacturing. Culture can be a much wider divide than is frequently realized in church communities. Just because we all speak the same language, for example, doesn't mean we have the same cultural roots or values. Church communities rarely address this regarding the official texts they use for worship, though it will sometimes find expression in the less-strictly policed area of musical styles.[1]

Depending on whether a community's texts are tightly controlled or open-ended will significantly affect the equivalent of the "director's" and "performer's" work. Rules, or other constraints or traditions, can be great aids to creativity. As Picasso supposedly said, "The picture is defined by the frame." JS Bach once limited himself to just five notes to see what he could create, and Stephen Sondheim once decided to compose only in waltz time (three-quarters-time) for an entire show (*A Little Night Music*). Boundaries can be our friends if we learn about their intention and purpose, their benefits (or lack of them!) and how to work with them. If you feel rules are only ever the enemy in your work, then the old advice still holds true: "Know your enemy very well!"

Always added to all of which is the ancient wisdom of all rule systems if one is completely committed to a course of action: "It is frequently easier to ask for forgiveness than permission."

The positive side of working with communities which have more rules is that they've probably done more work in helping us understand both what needs to happen and, most importantly, why it needs to happen within their scripts. The Roman Catholic Church's liturgical books, for example, are filled not just with a variety of scripts, but also introductions giving historical context, rubrics, as well as prompts for understanding intention and purpose within a prayer or section of the script, very similar to the prompts a director might give an actor. When present,

---

1. Musical copyright is a whole other matter and should be treated very carefully. Legal proceedings are very common where use, even accidental ones, without permission are discovered.

they're worth studying and sharing with the whole team. For any legalists among us, I recall one professor instilling into us the Roman tradition that "permissions are given in the general, denials are given in the specifics." This is worth remembering.

Frequently the rules as written have a lot more room for interpretation than how those rules have historically become "our local tradition" in a specific community. One of the great gifts of a good director is to see alternative ways of fulfilling the spirit (and even the letter) of the law than what has become "our way of doing it." People experience "our way of doing it" and believe it is the *only* way of fulfilling a specific requirement. One will frequently hear a director say in a rehearsal when questioned about intention or purpose, which church folk can learn to ask: "What does the script tell us?" for "the answer is always in the script." And to that, for church folks, I would certainly add "and the rubrics."

A good example of this may be found in the words of the US Conference of Roman Catholic Bishops' Liturgy Committee document entitled "Environment and Art in Catholic Worship" from 1978 (superseded in 2000 by "Built of Living Stones"). This short document is recommended for any worship team interested in the "why" of liturgy where, in paragraph four of the introduction, it says (emphasis added):

> Christians have not hesitated to use every human art in their celebration of the saving work of God in Jesus Christ, although in every historical period they have been influenced, at times inhibited, by cultural circumstances. In the resurrection of the Lord, all things are made new . . . *God does not need liturgy; people do, and people have only their own arts and styles of expression with which to celebrate.*

This last sentence was (and still is) a revelation to many. Yes, we are gathering to give glory to God, but not because God needs it. We are gathering because we need to remember our relationship with the creator of us and all things.

From both the view of a "director" and those ministering (the "actors") the fundamental recognition that the primary purpose of public acts of worship in the Christian tradition is to engage the congregation reminds us that the link between theater and worship is as real as ever. The purpose is always about providing a transformative experience for the people.

Of course, other faiths (and one thinks particularly of the more ancient Jewish Temple tradition) take different views, with elaborate rites laid out by what is believed to be divine revelation. But within Christianity, based on the Gospels, there is the minimal direction about how to remember Jesus by sharing bread and wine, with only one of the evangelists (Matthew, originally writing for a mainly Jewish community,) adding any specific motivation or intention from the Temple tradition of the forgiveness of sins. Noticeably Paul, in his letter to the Corinthians, our earliest text, along with Gospel writers Mark and Luke, don't mention this addition, and of course John doesn't even mention the bread or wine. Instead, John has Jesus wash the disciples' feet. Talk about a dramatic gesture worthy of a skilled theater director! John maybe felt that everyone already knew what Jesus said, for most scholars agree he was writing a few decades after the others, so there was no need to repeat it.

It may, alternatively, have been what John *wished* Jesus had done. No one else mentions the foot-washing, so some doubt exists. Either way, it's a story which continues to resonate through history. Isn't that what every preacher wishes they could create? As the ancient Hasidic proverb reminds us, "The truth is far too important to be left to mere facts." Symbolic actions are just as valid as symbolic words when trying to express an eternal truth.

Both these examples of storytelling—did Jesus mention forgiving sins at the Last Supper and/or wash the disciples' feet?—help us explore the intention and motivation of our liturgical scripts. They offer us the choice about how we wish to present them. Will we stick with what is held as The Tradition or ask other questions? If we accept that we're celebrating liturgy not because God needs it (for God needs nothing) but that we do, then maybe we can focus on asking questions which will help us as ministers be a source of nurture for our communities.

Alongside this we must remember that worship is not a solo event but, as Fr. Robert Rien, a pastor with whom I worked, always taught, "Communal liturgy is certainly personal, but it is not private." Balancing this communal and personal (though not private) gathering we call "liturgy" or "worship" is an art and a science, and as a worshipping community we're fortunate to have many centuries of experience and examples on which to draw if we did but search them out.

However, against this we have the very clear instructions of Jesus that when we pray (Mt.6:6) we should go somewhere private. When we put these two realities together, the resultant logic could challenge us to ask the question: Is Liturgy (communal experiences) primarily about prayer (private experiences) or something else? Or a balanced combination of the two? And if it's primarily about something else, what might that be?

And there, as Master Shakespeare reminds us, "is the rub."

When a director is asked to direct a play (or musical, movie, etc.), a range of "intentions" might be in their mind. A play can entertain, engage, awaken, educate, distract, inform, or challenge, among many other objectives. Noel Coward reminded us that the only unforgiveable sin was to bore the people, and that goes for worship too. The director's job is to decide on their intention by being deeply engaged with the script as well as the time, place, and context for the performance. They will usually also look to the historical context for the writing of the script (a topic to which we will return in Chapter 4), in case that gives rise to any useful information.

One well-known example of how time and place significantly impact a script's meaning is *The Crucible*, a play Arthur Miller wrote in 1953 during the McCarthy-era Anti-American Trials but set in the Massachusetts Bay Colony community of Salem during the witch trials of 1692–93. No mention of the contemporary 1953 trials is made in the play, but the exposure of the power of hysteria and group-think dysfunction makes Jesus' line of "whoever has ears, let them hear" (Mt. 13:9) seem implied. If a company chose to stage this play today, the history (both from 1692 and 1953) would need to be known by those involved, even if not referenced. The challenge would be to make all of that—the script, the historic contexts, the contemporary reality—present to a contemporary audience without giving them a two-hour lecture before the opening lines. This function of "making totally present an historical reality with a contemporary understanding" is, of course, a good description of what most worship leaders are trying to do every time they gather with their community for the Lord's Supper.

As for those who are called to be a director (or planner) for communal worship in Christian churches and then also to lead it, I think the full understanding of the purpose is in danger of being lost. It lays behind centuries of official Tradition and multiple little unofficial traditions, along the "I like it this way" lines of numerous clergy and congregants, and with the false notion that somehow God needs us to do it this way. To understand how to train well for the roles of being a worship director and/or presider and preacher we need to rediscover the truth that:

MEETING THE DIRECTOR AND PRODUCTION TEAM

- as with a play, we carry the huge responsibility, up to eight times a week (or more) as needed, of creating a moment of both communal transcendence and individual immanence, where each person present can have a personal experience alongside family, friends and strangers.
- that they are each invited to open themselves, (individually and communally) to the spirit of the piece so that it might enter and enlighten their hearts and minds.

In response to this, they may feel called to prayer, sing, dance, laugh, or all of the above. That's not our primary work. Our job is, to the best of our ability, to create the script, time and space where such a miracle can happen and, as the Buddhists teach, let go of the outcome.

A big transformation can happen in Christian worship when the leaders, even if they are the ones speaking, stop thinking they're praying on behalf of their community, and acknowledge that their primary work is to create a space and time where the congregation itself can pray. Theater teaches that it's about intention, and how changing that can change the voice which is speaking.

As a young Catholic adult I used a "Pope John Missal," which I still have, published in the UK in 1978. Prior to the "Order of Mass" there was a section in red, the color traditionally used for "the rubrics:"

> *Introductory Rites*
> *The Purpose of these rites is to help the assembled people to become a worshipping community and to prepare us to listen to God's word and to celebrate the eucharist.... Through the entrance song and the priest's greeting we become aware of the saving presence of Christ. We acknowledge that we are assembled in his name to worship the Father in his Spirit.*

For anyone working as worship leaders/presiders the "bits in red" are the voice of your director. An actor ignores their director at their own peril. Without it they become self-referential, which is rarely about serving others.

Whenever I attend a liturgical celebration (Catholic or otherwise), I remember these words in red. I'm always delighted if I feel that those who have planned the service and/or are leading it have worked consciously enough to make these critical first intentions happen, that the words and actions of what are technically called The Introductory Rites fulfill their purpose. We are told that a speaker has about thirty seconds to grab or lose their audience. This is true for visitors in church too, and even for the "regulars," for no one likes to be taken for granted.

As with a play, in liturgy there's a lot of work to do before even one word is spoken publicly. As the old King James bible reminds us in Proverbs 29:18, " Where there is no vison, the people perish." A director who has no vision, no intention, has little to offer to help an actor find their way through the text to the sub-text, and thence to meaning.

QUESTIONS FOR REFLECTION

For Presiders

1. Are you and the other "cast members" on the same page about the intention you're bringing to the script this time?
2. Pay attention to how varied and multi-faceted your "colleague cast members," including musicians, environment designers, lectors, etc., can be. Are you as flexible?
3. Are any of the cast (including you) "in a rut?" Is anyone just "phoning it in?" What effect does that have on the experience of worship?

For Preachers

1. Will your homily or sermon continue the purpose of the script, giving it voice, or not?
2. Are you in a rut in terms of your preaching style? Is the Word alive in you?
3. Do you notice the contributions other "cast members" make? Do you ever discuss with them how you can work together?

3

Knowing, Staying In, and Not Losing Yourself in Your Role (or Archetype)

An archetype held too tightly is like a bad actor, where the performance cries "look at me, I'm an actor and I'm acting." It happens in every profession at times.

A PERENNIAL QUESTION FOR all professionals is to what extent they work as themselves in their job. Are you ever off-duty? To what extent do your life, history, joys and pains, personal preferences, and experiences matter or should be allowed to change the way you perform your work? Different answers exist to this question, and what church leaders believe is the correct answer will influence how people are trained for ministry as we move through the 21st century.

Even with the advent of artificial intelligence, we aren't yet at a place where we want performative and ministerial facilitators to be non-human. We want them to be "one of us," even if they're also not just like us, and in some way "set apart" so that they can commune with both us and the gods/God. (See *ontological change* from the Preface.) For centuries, and certainly through to the 1950s, the idea of a "call" to ministry was very much about recognizing that a sense of "otherness" was going on for both stage and church.

When you're being an actor, you're literally "playing a part." You might find echoes of your character's situation in your own life, or your fantasy, or it might be completely "other." You may do research into their specific condition (alcoholic, homeless, a different ethnic group, social class, etc.), or how they walk, speak, or laugh.

Actors each have their own tricks for helping them find their character and their unique expression. I believe it was Dame Margaret Rutherford, a very popular portrayer of the crime-solving Miss Marple in the 1950s, who said, "Find the shoes and you've found the character!"

Whatever you decide, over the period of the rehearsals with your director and the rest of the cast, the end product the audience will see is not intended to be you. Maybe you feel that your gift of being able to relate to and inhabit these different people is part of your uniqueness in a world that wants to put each of us in a proverbial box. A person's ability to imagine living in a different skin, in a different story, potentially makes them powerful teachers in a world of "boxes."

When someone accepts the call to be a Christian minister, they're there very specifically and uniquely as themselves, as a whole person, with all their background, training, gifts, and faults. They're there with their family of origin traumas and cultural baggage, along with a unique journey through it all. This is what enables them to remain one of the community, able to be what Henri Nouwen calls a "wounded healer" in his amazing book of the same name.[1] They're also called to be willing to enter the other world of "time outside time" of the Divine and hold that reality present in their being too. When we are acting ritually in church, we have a similar set of supports to an actor in the theater (space, colleagues, special clothing, lights, music, etc.); but when we are, for example, at a sick person's bedside alone with the family, we must carry it all within ourself. Both callings must learn to be able to do the job with or without the props and settings. This is part of what it means to carry an archetype.

This word "archetype" usually relates to a role which has a common societal meaning or understanding. For our purposes, we'll define "archetype" as "the image and model of what the community needs that role to be." Different people will certainly do it differently, but as when we use the words "parent," "teacher," "president," etc., we're drawing on a communal understanding of what the role means, and what, within an acceptable range, anyone in that role is called to do and be.

---

1. Nouwen, *Wounded Healer*.

Whether as an actor (where "I" needs in some way to take second place to a constructed reality) or as a presider/preacher (where "I" needs to be distilled from just the personal into the trans-personal[2]), the individual is "not their ordinary self" when they're working. This isn't natural for most people, nor necessarily safe psychologically for some, and certainly never easy.

The big difference in the training between actors and clergy types is that actors, regardless of the "school" from which they come, take a lot of time learning how to "find" the character, the voice, the "other" within themselves, as well as how to communicate that "otherness" to an audience. They do this by practicing physical and mental skills over and over, doing scenes and productions, readings and numerous exercises, importantly with a mentor to watch and guide, instruct and affirm them. And then, as we have already noted, every show they ever do in their professional life will also have such a reference point, (a director,) to help shine a light on the path forward to discovery and communication through the rehearsal process.

A traditional Christian presider or preacher, on the other hand, who has gone through the Western seminary training for a Master of Divinity degree will spend very little time being helped (or, more importantly, being challenged) to "find their voice." If they have a good spiritual director they may be led to understand who they are in the process of taking on their archetype. Psychology and counseling will be studied and, hopefully, cast the theology student not only in the role of "provider" but also the client role of "seeker." Luckily, most are required to take one to three units of Clinical Pastoral Education, working as an assistant hospital chaplain or similar. This adds to, and is generally regarded as the toughest part of the entire five-year classical seminary process, because it challenges the individual to review their assumptions, biases, and prejudices, as well as their unresolved traumas and issues.

In other, more indigenous, traditions this would be the main topic of the entire seminary course, drawing learning out from these experiences, fears, and personal shadows, and letting these experiences be a starting point for much of the formal study of scripture, church history, moral theology, and the personal experience of the transcendent. To

---

2. Trans-personal we are defining as denoting or dealing with states or areas of consciousness beyond the limits of personal identity, often including a spiritual/divine connection.

"educate," after all, comes from the Latin *educare*, "to draw out," not to see how much new material the system can stuff back in.

Within living memory it was still suggested that there was little need for trainee clergy to practice this new skill set which was believed to be given automatically by the imposition of hands and anointing, as in the Jewish and Christian biblical models. What training they did need would be provided by being a junior minister in a parish under an experienced, older one. It rarely worked historically, and it doesn't work today, especially as ministers of less and less experience are put in positions of leadership.

Claiming the name of performer, presider, or preacher comes with accepting certain expectations. Those expectations, regardless of where someone is on the wide-ranging scale from beginner to mastery, mean one is submitting to being judged accordingly. We are saying, "This is who I accept I am in the world at this time." We carry many such names in a lifetime, though I suspect the only one we can all claim is "child." Many people are a "spouse" and/or a "parent," some a "leader" or another profession/vocation, such as "healer." These roles and sets of expectations interact as we move through life, and we must learn how we each will need to prioritize the requirements and expectations attached. In a lifetime we may carry several at the same time and, as most people have realized by the time they're in their mid-thirties, being a skilled juggler is often required!

Cultures have traditionally and wisely created special rituals or ceremonies to help individuals transition between or into new archetypes. Naming ceremonies, sometimes religious, start us off, though we have failed to maintain one for the major transition of becoming a parent. (It is a great shame that this very significant one is rather subsumed in the naming ceremony of the child. Would that we could change that!) When we graduate, when we marry, when we move into work leadership or management; many of these moments find a public celebration is appropriate. Why? Because it's not enough to say, "I think I'm now a . . ." It requires some sort of community to affirm this and say, "Yes, you are! We see you as that, and that in you!" This is why we clap at graduations, at weddings, and yes, even ordinations. Indeed, without a public affirmation, usually of applause, no Christian ordination is valid, no matter how many bishops and other clergy are present. This is also why in many countries marriage celebrations may not be legally held behind locked doors. These moments of transition are not just for the individual(s) involved but, even if only peripherally, the whole community.

ARCHETYPE HEALTH WARNING!

Having said this, it's also true that a person over-identifying with their role or archetype and forgetting who they are as a person is not psychologically healthy. This is true for any role or profession, from parents to professors, starlets to surgeons. The drive to be an "icon" in a society can come from the individual or from others, or some combination of the two. Some professionals have egos which aren't resolved and remain vulnerable. Similarly, society seems to want people on pedestals, if for no other reason than they are easy targets, scapegoats, to knock down when things go wrong, even if they aren't responsible.

Stories of unhealthy personalities over-identified with their status (commonly known as divas or divos) are found in all professions and certainly numerous in both the performing arts and churches. People have even made shows about them—one thinks particularly of the musical *Sunset Boulevard* with music by Andrew Lloyd Webber and lyrics by Don Black and Christopher Hampton, which was based on the 1950s movie of the same name directed by Billy Wilder and starring Gloria Swanson, among others.

The spiritual virtue of humility and the habit of remaining grounded requires constant nurturance and vigilance. This usually includes the role holder taking the initiative and removing themself from the spotlight and any false adulation. One thinks of Jesus taking time to retreat to the desert after the demands of the people, as well as wise ministers who write themselves out of town in their parish calendar. One friend uses the phrase "Going to the Desert Inn" when they need to find inner peace and quiet.

As much as all professions should be trained in how to deal with the demands of their work, they also need training in how to "let it go" and return to the normal realms, preferably without the misuse of alcohol or other drugs.

Parish and community ministers should also take a note of how many archetypes they're juggling, and which one is appropriate at any one time. As we mentioned in chapter 1, within any 24-hour period a Christian minister may be a counselor, an agent of social justice, a promotions manager, and team leader, as well as a spouse and parent in some cases. All of these can be demanding functions and require different gifts. However, when we swap tasks, are we aware of the conscious need to swap archetypes too? When we're presiding, are we there as minister of the Good News, or as a parent or team leader? When we're preaching, are we there as a counselor or the budget committee chair rather than as someone invited to break open the Word of God? All our tasks and experiences can count and be useful in our ministry, but being able to know "as whom am I standing here now?" matters very much too.

As with a performer, liturgical ministers in leadership roles need to ask themselves if they're willing to commit the time, training, and energy needed to take the role seriously. Rather like a marriage vow, which a vocation can so easily be, are we willing to, if not "forsake all others," at least know and be clear and explicit about where our priorities are based?

With these warnings in mind, what might be the main elements of the largely unwritten contract between each of these archetypes and their communities?

THE PERFORMER ARCHETYPE

Historically the performer stands with one foot in the "storyteller" camp and the other in the realm of "wizards and sorcerers." Consequently, actors have alternatively been honored and hounded throughout history. Some have also suggested that actors are priests too, needed to help the audience transcend the limits of time and space. Antonin Artaud, along with Jerzy Grotowski, referred to the "holy actor" as being needed to enable an audience to transcend the ordinary to reach the realm of magical reality.[3]

In ancient Greece and Rome, the play was an entertainment for the gods as much as for the humans, and incense was often burned at the beginning to honor them and invite them in, making it a formal part of worship, especially for the Feast of Dionysius. This was the situation which brought about the initial separation between nascent Christianity and the performing arts, with theater seen as a form of pagan worship with the actors as if not actual priests, certainly as acolytes. Appeals to "magical reality" and the ability to represent the gods didn't help either.

---

3. The approach by Artaud and Grotowski to theater as a sacred art form is well explored in *Performing the Sacred*, 44–49, by Todd E. Johnson & Dale Savidge. Many other references are also given there which might be useful to those unfamiliar with the performing arts as a ministerial skill set.

However, whether it is for laughter or tears, an audience wants the acting company to "transport" them to a different place and/or time. An actor is a storyteller, and every culture needs to tell its stories to remember who it is and explore who it wishes to become. An actor isn't a newscaster, although they may deal in historical reality. Similarly, an actor isn't a journalist, though there might be a certain amount of reportage in a script. The actor's job is to so effectively become the characters of a story that we forget who they are and where we are in this alternative reality for a while, feeling all the feelings of these beings who live lives we do not. While today we'd regard a review that said a certain performer "cast a spell on the audience" as a good thing, it's worth remembering that history was not always so accepting.

Things a performer might want to hear after a performance include mesmerizing, touching, engaging, hypnotic, transformative, cathartic, entertaining, hysterical, energizing, powerful, and other-worldly. Here we can see qualities that are also used to describe religious or spiritual gatherings. However, what a contemporary actor or other performer is not trying to do, even if they're telling a religious story, is primarily to create a spiritual experience or engage the audience in religious worship. It might happen that some of the audience find a scene or a whole play spiritual or worshipful, but it's not usually part of the planning or the intention of the piece. An actor is dealing with the human dimensions, not the divine, focusing on the secular and not any potential transcendent or religious meaning of a script.

This doesn't mean that the audience can't take away spiritual lessons or feel that they've been at a religious event; it's just not the intention. The possible exceptions to this are the Passion and Morality plays of the medieval period and beyond, right up to the continuing tradition in the village of Oberammergau in Bavaria, Germany and their Passion Play, performed in response to an oath to God every ten years since 1634.[4]

Good examples of plays which deal with religious or spiritual issues but are not acts of worship include *Saint Joan* by George Bernard Shaw, *A Man for all Seasons* by Robert Bolt, and of course *Murder in the Cathedral* by T.S. Eliot. Contemporary musicals like *Godspell* and *Jesus Christ*

---

4. The extensive Passion, Mystery and Everyman Play Cycles of Europe are still performed and reinvented. Most scripts have been lost but some early ones are available dating from the 14th and 15th centuries. Still given performances in the UK are plays from the York, Wakefield, Hereford, Coventry and Chester cycles. For more information see, for example, the Radius (Religious Drama Society of Great Britain) website https://www.radiusdrama.org.uk.

Superstar come to mind too. Similarly, a performance of Bach's Mass in B Minor, Elgar's "Dream of Gerontius" or Handel's "Messiah" can be given to significant spiritual as well as musical benefit without the performers having any commitment to faith, even though the composers might have. What all these pieces share is a masterful script or manuscript, where the words or notes can, manifested in the right body with breath, carry more than just temporal meaning.

Neither an actor nor acting company, nor a musician or whole symphony orchestra and chorus, are working on these pieces because they're about religious lives but because they're about human lives. The performer(s) might or might not "believe" in saints and eternal life; their job is to bring the script (or manuscript) to life under the guidance of the director, musical or otherwise. While one might be encouraged to explore the religious and spiritual life of the character to play the part, you don't need to believe the same in your own life. Having said that, it is also worth recalling the story of Balaam's donkey (Num 22:21–39) as a useful reminder that the Word will find a way to speak when the message needs to find a voice. Even an inexperienced ass can have their moment!

In the late 1970s at an event for Radius, the Religious Drama Society of Great Britain in London UK, the speaker said, in effect, "There is no such thing as good or bad religious art—art is not religious. It might have a religious theme, but in and of itself, it is not religious. Art is either good or bad."

Unfortunately, a lot of bad art is allowed in churches because it is "religious," as if that was an excuse for low standards or poor technical ability. This might be true for some occasions (like youth Sunday) but not on a regular basis. We might forgive well-intentioned though not well-executed art more easily in some situations, like we do a middle school play or music recital, but it doesn't make it good. Anyone carrying an archetype is at some level committed to striving to carry it well, to become more skilled at their craft. The performing we're talking about here is not what children do to explore their ego limits or identity, or work out power dynamics between siblings. We're talking about carrying the archetype for the good of the community and, in that sense, Artaud was correct—actors, like healers, teachers, and parents, do touch on the sacred and therefore the archetype of the priest too.

Actors might be trained in the Stanislavski Method, the Meisner Technique, by following the ideas of Method Acting, or by just watching others and then making it up as you go along. As a performer the job is basically two-fold: To work out what's going on inside the character (feelings—especially loves and fears—secrets, wants, perceptions, etc.) and if (and then how and when) to physically reveal this sub-text in the process of the script, so that the audience can become engaged, stay engaged, and want to travel with you for the remaining time before the final curtain, and maybe even afterwards.

The job of a performer is to marshal natural gifts and learned skills and set them at the service of the script or manuscript, and then get out of the way so that the audience can have the experience of what the author intended. The audience isn't paying to watch us actors have an experience, though we may. They're paying so that they can have an experience and take it home with them. This is delightfully exemplified by the perfectly delivered comment comedian Steve Martin once made when introducing Meryl Streep at an awards show: "She makes us think, and we resent her for it.⁵"

The ultimate gift of a good performer is generosity, even if it's with a gift we don't want (in the form of inviting us into a self-revelation) or that will make our life more complicated. Performers dig into themselves and lay what they find out in the open so that the audience can see themselves mirrored back. The director's job is to ensure it's all done in the service of the script and remains appropriate and useful to the arc of the production. The performer's job is to do the work of self/character discovery and revelation, and not worry about the editing, which happens (we hope) in the rehearsal process.

At some level, and to different degrees, all this is what one carries as the archetype when one claims, or is given, the title of performer. To be an artist in any discipline is to undertake a life journey, made up of many smaller journeys, and not to be settled when one arrives at any one port.

THE PRESIDER ("PRIEST") ARCHETYPE

Most modern definitions of the noun "priest" focus on someone having the authority to perform or authorize religious rites, though the Merriam-Webster Dictionary definition also includes "especially as a mediatory agent between humans and God." Other words that are associated with this function in different cultures include shaman, medicine worker

---

5. A friend suggested that the sub-title for this book be "How Would Meryl Streep Say Mass?" It was considered, briefly.

or medium. In Judaism the tribe of Levi, the family and male descendants of Moses' brother Aaron, was set aside by God to serve as priests for the whole people. The words "set aside," "called by God," "anointed," and "intermediary" are common when talking about the role of priests, rabbis, pastors, and other religious leaders in a society. It is not always a "once and done" call and may only be considered operational in some cultures when the person is, for example, wearing certain clothes, masks, or robes, or in some type of trance, or if they are doing their work in a specific place or circumstance.

Although not roles created by Jesus, who only called disciples (who then graduated to apostles after Pentecost), by the fourth or fifth century bishops, priests, and deacons were universal throughout the Christian world, reflecting the priestly traditions of Judaism as well as other Mediterranean religions. The consistent teaching that people don't need an "intermediary" to approach the Divine which Jesus had established had been at least paralleled, and in some places completely superseded, by the requirement for a special cultic leadership. This leadership continued to be defined as being "separate" and "special" and frequently implied by comparison that "regular people" lack this link to heaven, which was a boon for job security. However, to be fair "regular Christian people," just like the Hebrews in the desert at Mount Horeb before them, were and are often fearful of being spoken to directly by the Divine (Deut 18:15-20). Christian clergy, while affirming the direct access available to all, remain for many a route for intercession and negotiation with their God.

These traditional definitions were radically shifted in the Western world by the Reformation. Looked at objectively, it's still challenging to separate a contemporary Christian leader who performs liturgical rites from those Reformation accusations, especially when many are still using rituals and words directly mirroring the ones used over 500 years ago, even if not in Latin and behind a rood screen. We still seem to suggest that "priests" can take ordinary things from the store or someone's kitchen (like bread and wine, and even maybe water, candles, and oil) and, in their hands (and *only* their hands), when saying certain words and doing certain gestures, they become not just symbols (which most people can accept quite readily) but deeper signifiers and even (in a sacramental way) the thing itself, particularly the body and blood of the risen Christ. (See *transubstantiation* and *consubstantiation* from the Introduction.) This claim, because it is impossible to verify scientifically, might be equally made by those leading pagan rituals as it is by ritualistic

Christianity. Part of the challenge of effectively inhabiting the archetype of liturgical leader ("priest") in the twenty-first century is owning up to this reality. From the pre-Reformation perspective, theologians Augustine of Hippo mentioned earlier and Thomas Aquinas OP, (1225—1274), basing their thought on that of the Greek philosopher Aristotle, (384-22 BCE), offered inventive work on the "substance and accidents" of matter and tried to explain why the mystery of the Eucharist is not actually magic. However, many remained—and remain—unconvinced. (Roughly only about 30 percent of Catholics in the US, for example, believe in transubstantiation according to the latest Pew Research, even though their church has not changed any of its teaching.[6])

It's a shame we couldn't accept a simpler line of explanation and just say something like, "This is what Jesus said, as far as we know, at what we call the Last Supper, and what the very earliest Christian community (followers of The Way) celebrated (1 Cor 11:23-26). Because Jesus said it, we believe it, and when we do it, we also experience it, like those earliest followers. But we can't explain it; it's a wonderful mystery. And that's okay!" It's a transcendent reality which is unique, and there's an argument to suggest that we should be fine to simply say, "It is what it is, and it is beyond words, just like love."

As liturgical leaders we should be encouraging people to trust the levels of mystery in the actions of love made flesh. Do them. Experience them. Trust them. But don't try and reduce them to explanatory words. Being willing and able to live in the mystery, I would suggest, is what the archetype of priesthood (as opposed to lecturer, therapist, or counselor) is about.

Such appeals to "mystery" were much more acceptable and therefore normal before the Reformation, before the scientific revolution and the internet age. Most if not all ancient and indigenous peoples accepted and celebrated a dimension of reality that wasn't physical and wasn't sustained or controlled by physical laws. The existence of this additional or "other" reality or realm was a place where God or the gods dwelt, and where ordinary people could visit, or maybe hope to go to after death. Priests were the people who could help the community connect with and experience this place. Whether one was hoping for Heaven, Valhalla, or the Field of Reeds ruled by Osiris for worthy Egyptians, ministry for the priest in such cultures was to help people to live so as both to bring that future reality

6. https://www.pewresearch.org/short-reads/2019/08/05/transubstantiation-eucharist-u-s-catholics/.

to the present as well as become part of those "saved" (to use a Christian word,) in the next. Priesthood has very little unique about it when it's divorced from the "otherness" of that which is beyond the material.

The amazing thing is that even in a contemporary world where people are withdrawing from organized religions at a record-shattering rate, belief in, or at least a hope for, "something else" is almost as great as ever. Who knows, maybe discoveries in quantum mechanics or AI will provide us justification for revisiting "the good old days" of belief in the unseen.

These days people may describe themselves as "spiritual but not religious," or "nones", and while that can be a cop-out for not doing the work of a more rigorous spiritual discipline, it's also a very similar opening to the "altar to an unknown god" on which the apostle Paul famously capitalized when in Athens (Acts 17:23). Some human beings do tend, it seems, to be open to the otherness of what we might call the spiritual, metaphysical, or otherworldly. What we can't say is that science has turned people away from mystery and wonder. In fact, while what "we know" has certainly increased significantly since the time of Jesus, what science has shown us is that what we *don't* know has increased even more. Postmodern humanity has re-learned to hold unknowing, and to ask the "what if?" of the space where "something" exists which is not yet definable. This is, in consequence, a fertile and exciting time for priesthood. Or at least it could be if we approach this "unknowing" humbly and generously, not pretending to understand or control it but willing to embrace and celebrate it, and then to help people experience it. The challenge with this approach is that it requires us to trust in God and the action of the Spirit in life.

Possibly one of the big failures of Christian leadership has been to ask for belief in doctrine which explains (often unsatisfactorily) mystery, rather than help people experience the mystery which is beyond dogma. That's not to say we shouldn't try to put words to our experiences, nor to help us understand the doctrine, but one can make the argument that the balance between these functions has been "out of whack" for centuries. (The late Fr. James Brand always said, "theology is the love words of the bride for the bridegroom." When it moves beyond poetry into facts and statistics, it's on dangerous territory.)

It's interesting that whoever was first telling the story of what became the Book of Genesis located the failure of connection between the Divine and humans in our "need to know everything," rather than living the experience of trust and faith. Adam and Eve eat from the Tree of the

Knowledge of Good and Evil, a function which the Creator had reserved for Godself. To counter this, at each stage of the story thereafter the "righteous" person acts in trust even through the experience of not understanding—Abraham being asked first to leave home and then to sacrifice Issac, Moses at the Red Sea, Job enduring his trials, right through to Mary saying to Gabriel, "Let it be according to your word," which her son Jesus recapitulates as "your will not mine be done" in Gethsemane.

Liturgical leadership is called to stand in the unknowing and trust, in faith and mystery, in the hope of wonder and awe. As an actor would say, "trust the script!" One can still be doing great and good work as a counselor, therapist or mentor, all vital and healing, if one isn't standing there, but it just isn't carrying the archetype of priesthood. Alternatively, when someone is standing in that place, even if they aren't ordained, they're carrying it.

In order to experience mystery and wonder today, people read or go for walks in nature, go to the theater, or watch TV or movies. Too few still expect to engage wonder and awe on a regular basis in a liturgical church. Has contemporary priesthood set the bar too low for that apparently innate capacity for the unknown, even as we acknowledge that the way we understand ourselves has changed—and is changing—significantly? One hopes not, given the pace at which our knowledge is growing about quantum physics, chaos theory, and much more. For those who will not believe unless they understand, more "unknowns" exist in our future than in our past. Experiencing and accepting a world of Spirit is relatively easy by comparison, if we're open to it. But it has to be modelled with integrity, or it will not be attractive. If the leaders don't act as if they believe, why should anyone else?

THE PREACHER ARCHETYPE

This archetype is associated with the functions of wisdom-giver, teacher, and one who can articulate the voice of the Divine for the ears of mortals. It relates strongly, though usually only occasionally, with the role of prophet. Most preachers will never be overtly prophetic in the sense of breaking open a new message or warning, but their ability to communicate more mundane messages (which must be repeated for each generation, each community, each person, sometimes more than once) is nonetheless critical. Preaching, which is, to repeat, the hardest of liturgical ministries, requires two distinct gifts, those of composition and delivery. Even minimal competency requires work and inspiration.

It is said that each of us only really has one or two actual homilies (or sermons) in us, so that we must find numerous different ways to unpack it at each telling. The unique gift of the preacher therefore is not so much the actual message (as in a prophecy) but how to express it in such a way as it can be heard, understood, integrated, and internalized for each community and individual over time. Unfortunately, such a role and an archetype or charism isn't particularly appreciated or encouraged in many Caucasian churches or seminaries as its own gift or call. If you're called to the diaconate or priesthood, the assumption is you can obviously preach, right? Wrong!

The Reformed churches have understood this for much longer than the Catholic and Orthodox churches, thanks to the pioneers who fought to "wake up" their older siblings of faith from their 1,400-year-old habits. A further 500 years (until the Second Vatican Council) passed for Catholicism to admit that the lesson needed to be learned, though only limited success has followed the work which has been done so far to implement any changes.

When you hear bishops (including those of Rome) and seminary professors saying one should never speak for more than eight to ten minutes, because people these days don't have a sufficient attention span, what they're really saying is, "You're probably not a good enough preacher to spin out the message for longer, so get up, say your bit, and sit down." Of course, a good homily or sermon can certainly be done in eight minutes or even less, and if you don't have the gift of being a preacher, brevity is a good rule to follow. It's an honest admission that your gifts lay in other areas. However, to say that sermons should never be longer than eight to ten minutes is like saying to an actor that plays should never take more than a similar timespan, or to a trained dancer that a ballet should be over in that space too. It's saying you're not good enough at your craft to undertake and sustain the audience's interest in a longer piece. Most Reformed churches would be appalled if the sermon were this short. They would feel cheated. And they'd expect it to be good too!

While speaking, especially for more than ten minutes, requires work, it should be, if not immediately the norm, certainly a goal to reach for. The problem of not prioritizing the role or gift (archetype) of preacher is exacerbated if it's seen in someone who isn't ordained or "called." Consequently, churches don't generally offer other people the skills training needed. This is both sad and worrisome, putting more emphasis on the ritual action of the presider to carry the message of the day. The problem is that the presider has very little control over the script, while the preacher does.

Someone who carries the archetype of preacher will be diligent in doing the groundwork, in prayer and study, and then in openness to the Spirit for the new thing being spoken today, now. They'll also be a person of experience, of both the ups and downs of life, and probably have a few years of therapy or spiritual mentorship under their belt. The words of St. Ignatius of Loyola will resound in the preacher's preparation: "Be scrupulously concerned about the truth of your experience, no matter where the truth might lead."[7] The "ah-ha" of a good homily or sermon is always lifegiving, even if that means engaging an "uh-oh" of a truth beforehand.

Like a skilled actor preparing a monologue, a preacher will do their research, maybe writing their thoughts down, and engage in conversations with colleagues (as an actor would the director and other actors) and with the silence in the words. Well-regarded preachers will often implement a similar process prior to delivery by engaging their mind, their heart, and their inspired intuition. Like an actor, the preacher is expected to speak with passion and depth, to be vulnerable and in the moment, taking the congregation on a journey into the message and the meaning.

The archetype of preacher is probably best exemplified by examples, so one thinks of people like Dr. Martin Luther King Jr., Archbishop Rowan Williams of Canterbury and Mother Theresa of Calcutta. As with a good actor, one wants to be left moved and engaged by a preacher. The following quote from *St. Francis and the foolishness of God* is pertinent in this regard:[8]

> *The essence of the prophetic task is to articulate a vision of the common good that has the power to capture the imagination of the people as a goal worthy of struggle and sacrifice.*

All three roles of performer, preacher and presider share the reality that they simultaneously exist in a trinity of environments or relationships: With the author (Divine or otherwise), with the culture, and with the individuals who make up a specific audience or congregation. These

---

7. Paragraph 12.99 of *St. Ignatius' Own Story*, translated by William J. Young.

8. *St. Francis and the Foolishness of God* by Marie Dennis, Cynthia Moe-Lobeda, Joseph Nangle, and Stuart Taylor, (Maryknoll, NY: Orbis Books, 1993, 2015), 5–6, 6–7. Quoted by Richard Rohr OFM, CAC, Daily Meditation, 9/6/2023.

three relationships are where the three essential elements mentioned in the Prologue find their home: intention, words having meaning, and the practitioners having a body with breath in time and space.

ARCHETYPES IN RELATIONSHIP TO THE AUTHOR

All performers, presiders, and preachers first and foremost exist in a relationship with the author of the work they're presenting. This is the source of the intention which guides our work. This relationship with the source needs to be carefully and diligently nurtured, whether it just concerns one element of their creation (a specific play, a certain song, one theme of revelation) or their whole catalogue and person.

Most performers rarely get to speak directly with their author, and when they do, it's a high point of a career for many. Most of the time they're working through research, stories of past presentations, and their own and the director's intuition and inspiration. (We will discuss this further in Chapter 4.) Presiders and preachers do much the same but have the added opportunity to build a relationship with the Divine author of their work over a lifetime.

An audience does not expect a performer to have an ongoing, intimate personal relationship with, say, Shakespeare or Rachmaninoff. A congregation does expect their presiders and preachers to have such with the Creator. When the artist performs, they're not performing to or for their author but for the audience. When a presider or preacher does their job, they are very much expected to be speaking and acting with, for, and by the power of their author. The Christian presider spends much of their script speaking directly to the Divine on behalf of the congregation. The preacher will be addressing the congregation but also trying to carry the message of the Author. This is why we talk about these roles being exercised "*in persona Christi*."

Practitioners of all three vocations have occasionally spoken about the feeling of "channeling" their author or character, which must be wonderful when it happens. For most of us being willing to take the time and do the work, to have the habits appropriate to our role, and to "trust the process" of preparation and the moment of presentation is the issue.

To be a true exponent of any of these archetypes, one ultimately needs to have a discipline of continual training and commitment, but especially the humility to surrender to the creator and creation on which we're working. We deeply engage the author so that we can speak with their authority.

ARCHETYPES IN RELATIONSHIP WITH THE CULTURE

The famous remark that "Britain and America are two countries separated by a common language" has been various attributed to George Bernard Shaw and Oscar Wilde (interestingly both Irish playwrights), as well as to Winston Churchill. Whoever first came up with the line, the wisdom is sufficiently accurate to quote. Most of the time it doesn't matter, but every now and again, a word or phrase just doesn't "land" correctly, and then confusion (and sometimes humor) ensues. This is because words find their meaning not in the dictionary but in the culture which uses them.

While we can claim there is evidence that the world's indeed becoming a smaller place, cultural differences remain, even within one country. Whether we're talking about words, music, styles of decoration and art, popular images, or cultural norms, we still remain a community of villages, tied to ideas which our "group" holds tightly. Or, as Tony Kushner commented of America in his play *Angels in America*, ". . . it's a melting pot in which nothing melts."

Our three archetypes all have unique historical relationships with different cultural contexts, and those cultures can be within small, tight areas (like either sides of a set of railway tracks or a river) or across great areas of a country or even continent. Think of yourself walking into a bar, café or diner in various towns and answering the question "what do you do?" with "I'm a pastor," or whatever is appropriate, and the reaction you would get. You'll be immediately matched up with the image the other person has of your "type." Do they know anyone else who does that? If so, what do they think of them? What are their prejudices or stereotypes?

In the same way words, images, and styles of communication can shift significantly as one travels, resulting in communication being stilted and limited. As we mentioned earlier, even the difference between city and rural culture, about where one was born and where one is called to work, can impact the results.

Traveling arts companies (theater groups, bands, dance companies) take these issues seriously when planning their tours and programming, and indeed sometimes assume they won't sell many tickets in certain towns. Different language and cultural styles of church are similarly called forth by different groups. All three archetypes are called to engage the culture of an area yet also to speak out and challenge it in some ways. Therefore, the decision must be made about what's negotiable and what isn't in order to get the job done. Where might there be flexibility in the language of the role and where might there be none? If we don't have a living relationship with the culture, especially if we come from a much different one, our work can be significantly hampered.[9]

ARCHETYPES IN RELATIONSHIP TO THE LOCAL INDIVIDUALS AND COMMUNITY

Finally, we must also examine briefly what the dimensions of these archetypes are when we're working and living in the community. They largely follow assumptions and the natural resistance to change. They include:

- People's assumptions about what a performer or presider/preacher should do and say when out and about in the community
- Assumptions about how they should interact with the local community

For performers, unless a person is particularly famous and recognizable, this isn't a large issue, for they can easily hide in the community if they wish. Alternatively, if you're ordained in a church or are an official in one, congregants will assume you'll follow the script as laid out in your church's liturgical and other books. If different options exist for what to do, the local assumption is probably that you'll make the same choices as the last person.

Assumptions will be made that you have a lifestyle in accordance with church rules and more particularly the community's expectations, including your style of dress, the friends you keep, your close relationships (including spouse if allowed), and the car you drive, and that you will be available as needed, certainly at least as much as the last pastor. Assumptions will be made that your priorities for the community (social,

---

9. The topic of the interface of culture and faith was the life's work of Dr. Joseph Martos, whose influence continues for many in the liturgical churches. From his seminal *Doors to the Sacred* to the final synthesis of his work in *Honest Rituals, Honest Sacraments*, Dr. Martos lived and worked in the space which honored a continuous dialogue between the Divine Author and our interpretation. Both these books should be required for any minister working in a liturgical church.

pastoral, liturgical, structural, financial) will align with those of the parish council and stay within the finance budget.

While some parishioners will have kept up with their faith development and will have integrated it into their life experiences as they aged, others (usually the majority) will assume that what you believe about the Divine Other after anywhere between three years and a lifetime of in-depth study and prayer is pretty much what they still believe after a short series of confirmation classes between thirty and sixty years ago when they were twelve years old.

Assumptions will be made about "where God is" when people have been taught to pray for hundreds of years by looking to the front and up—or down—with eyes open or closed. Assumptions will be made about what's required for a sacrament to happen and whether it really matters or not. Basically, assumptions will be made about pretty much everything, and it will matter because for many people the archetype you carry is to fulfill their expectations. A priest or liturgical minister should be what they think a minister should be. Similarly, post-churched and non-churched folks also won't lack in expectations and assumptions, especially after the sex and financial scandals of the past generation or two.

All these assumptions are, we can see, about what a person will do and how they'll do it. They aren't about who the person is while they do it. As one priest put it to me: "Our tradition says I am a priest chosen by God for service to God's people by celebrating the sacraments. People, when they don't like what I do or say, seem to have no problem suggesting God got it wrong."

If there once was a time when, rightly or wrongly, the clergy (or the clergy-adjacent) carried such a strong archetype in the community that they could do no wrong and would be almost unquestionably believed and obeyed, that time has long gone. It seems it might be time for each community or tradition to renegotiate their common understanding of the archetype for the new ways of being church, in the twenty-first century. The challenge will be to do so in a manner that recognizes that an archetype is not the same as just a role or job. It carries a level of "being" and not just "doing," and is as much about nature as ability.

IN CONCLUSION

Relevant for both presider and preacher, each generation must discover a new way of carrying one or both archetypes. The new way is not only a process concerning mediation with a God who was defined once, thousands of years ago, and cemented in tradition, but with one who is still self-revealing. This is especially true if we wish to engage in evangelism and outreach to the nones and others. The archetypes need to minister in the name of the Godself today, and not just in the exegesis of sacred scripture. After all, whatever's known of that which we call "God" is just a fraction of whatever is still to know. We must find what it means to be "called" to be in relationship with the wonderful "unknown" of the undefinable experience and relationship that we attempt to inadequately contain in the little word "God," or in alternatives such as "Divine Other," "The Ground of our Being," etc. We must simultaneously be a little mad, trusting wanderers and, most importantly, faithful lovers who remain constant to that relationship.

To be called is very similar to being a performer, often summoned to be in the mind of a creator (author, composer, choreographer) of another time and country, yet to find the meaning and relevance for today and this place. We must know who we are and what we're called to do as well as be, and bring all our skill and experience to bear. We must face up to the fact that, in our search, we may take wrong turns and hit dead ends. We must then surrender to the wonder of the moment, the relationships and the gifts which are wrapped in the work. Finally, we must hold sacred both types of Sabbaths—the focus-day(s) of our liturgical work, and our days off!

QUESTIONS

1. How do I relate to the archetype of my job? Can I separate it from my work? (If you're not sure what your work is, take a look at your calendar.)

2. Do I consciously carry my archetype all the time, or just when I'm doing liturgical and/or sacramental ministry? Are there definite times when I take it off or put it down?

3. If you add up all the time you spend doing what only you as someone who carries your archetype can do (as opposed to all the other jobs you do), including preparation and training time, what proportion of your week would that be?

4. Jesus asked the disciples "who do people say that I am?" (Mt. 16:13). Who do people say that you are? Should you believe them? Are they correct?

4

The Historical and Cultural Context of the Script

Understanding the Roles of the Dramaturge and Liturgist

Some ministers seem more concerned with the script than how the words are communicated, preferring historical rectitude over the needs of contemporary proclamation.

WHETHER ONE IS PRODUCING a piece of drama or a liturgy, neither happens without both a contemporary and an historical script and context which involve social relationships and expectations, conventions and influences. However, it may be that only a few people on the team and in the audience or congregation are aware of any, let alone all, of these influences. A theater company can stage a production of Chekov's *The Cherry Orchard* just as a church community and ministers can gather for a service from a prayer book or sacramentary and take everything in either script at face value. However, while such naïve productions may find much newness in their fulfillment of the text (and that's a real blessing at times), chances are they'll fail to plumb the potential depths of either. Of course, that all the participants were totally naïve about the script would be unlikely. One can assume that a theater director has at least some experience, or access to the internet, in order to draw on the background of a play and its author. Similarly, anyone with the title of liturgical planner, presider or preacher can be assumed to have spent some time studying scripture and their tradition to be accredited with the title. However, I can attest that, while almost all ministers and theater directors have some training, many don't have much in the particular area of exploring the full panoply of potential options available to each as they incarnate a script into being a living, engaged reality.

But there is good news! Help is at hand!

The name for the person who helps shepherd the respective production is either a dramaturge in the theater or a liturgist in the church. Their function, even if they're also members of the company (actor, musician, presider), is to speak from "outside" of the production. In both cases they bring research and education from beyond the immediate talent needed by a particular production. Both support and serve the creative process while seeing the event in the wider context of, for example, how this piece has been done in the past, what the social mores written into the text and subtext of the script are, and (particularly if the historical nature of the event is being updated in any way) what are the parallel social structures which come into play between then and now. These points of entry and development are as relevant for liturgy as they are for the theater.

The Merriam-Webster Dictionary defines dramaturgy as "the art or technique of dramatic composition and theatrical representation." Liturgy, on the other hand, is defined in part as "a rite or body of rites prescribed for public worship." What separates these nouns for many is that, while drama is seen as being all about the new and different, an assumption of what I once heard called "the tyranny of the 'ought'" is leveled against the latter, as if liturgy was just understanding a series of "you ought" (aka "one should" or "everyone must") and has no space for taking a moment to breathe and contemplate something new. The old, sad joke about the difference between a liturgist and a terrorist (A: "You can negotiate with a terrorist") is, hopefully, no longer as valid as it's been in the past.

A good liturgist doesn't just know what the rubrics say but also why they say it, what such and such a direction is meant to convey and, maybe most importantly, whether this action or rite has a different social and/or contemporary equivalence in this culture and time as opposed to the time and place for which it was originally designed. This is what we could call an attentiveness to enculturation and what Dr. Martos might call a search for the honest and true.

A piece of theater doesn't usually come with such apparently strict limitations, though many times in history the attitude of "we've always done it that way" has plagued the creativity of the stage as much as the church. The operettas of Gilbert and Sullivan are an excellent example of a series of works which for decades were encapsulated in their original productions, where they ossified almost to death. Alternatively, the plays of William Shakespeare have managed to survive being restaged, translated, updated, and re-formatted (including as musicals, ballets, operas, and movies) many times. Admittedly some work better than others, while some fail miserably. However, I would contend that the presence of "oughts," either written or cultural, are to be taken with a grain of salt, and with the understanding that, though it once resided in the single mind of someone, that might not be relevant for the new moment and place.

The job of the dramaturge and the liturgist includes helping a company or team discuss and appreciate all the nuances of all appropriate influences and come to a conscious, deliberate decision, and not be at the direction of any unconscious "ought" left behind from previous productions. The "unconscious ought" should be worked with until it becomes the "conscious choice."

Here we come to a potential conflict between what's considered normal with theater companies (that each time a script is re-created it has the possibility, indeed expectation, of being in some way re-imagined), and what is normal in a church, where the word "ritual" is often used instead of "liturgy," itself implying a repetition and consistency of form and words whose function is (hopefully) to re-create liminal reality outside time and space.

Pick your dictionary of choice, and you'll find a definition for "ritual" something like that of the Cambridge English Dictionary: "A set of actions or words performed in a regular way, often as part of a religious ceremony. A ritual is also any act done regularly, usually without thinking about it." And there we have the challenge: How do we keep a ritual recognizable and familiar, and thus facilitate participation and an openness within the congregation to receiving the gifts available in the process, while at the same time not causing it to become something that feels mindless and rote? This balancing act has always been difficult and is best remedied by the idea of "tradition" also being something that can be alive, that can shift with time and experience (which brings us back to Tevye and Golda facing the same question in *Fiddler on the Roof*).

In "the good old days" Christian religious tradition just said, "If you don't come to church when we say so, you'll go to hell," and that worked for many centuries, with no regard for keeping the content in any way relevant or current. After all, God doesn't change, so why should anything else? However, in spite of the earnest and dedicated work of many men and women over the centuries, (for example Catherine of Siena who challenged the "stuck-ness" of Western Christianity in her time,) being able to fall back on threats of "hellfire and damnation," even when it was well-meant, did very little to improve the skill level of the practitioners. Unfortunately, it did a lot to increase the individual and communal sense of power and importance of these leaders, as well as their lack of openness to criticism and growth. The tyranny of the "ought" ruled! While pointing the finger at the leadership of the Roman Catholic church on this issue is easy, many other post-Reformation churches have, over the more recent years, used the threat of hell and the immutableness of their words and (basically man-made) rites to turn living ritual into stone, and then used this stone to grind down the spirit of the people.

The reality of the twentieth and even more so the twenty-first centuries is firstly that people feel no need to believe in hell anymore as a place after death, for we have created it on earth more than once, and many people globally (if not most) live in some form of it every day, even though they have done nothing to deserve it. To be of interest, the "Good News" has to offer something else. Secondly, as mentioned above, that modern cultural change is measured in an ever-shrinking number of years rather than by a century or two, (The Middle Ages, the Renaissance, etc.) is clearer now than ever before.

Tradition has to become a living thing if it's to retain its relevance for each new audience. That's not to say millennials can't appreciate a liturgy in the Tridentine tradition or a Bach sonata on original instruments. What we shouldn't accept, however, is that there is *only one way* to appreciate and engage with either. Educated and liberated people (which, again, much of the world is still not, in spite of the efforts of many heroic people) will certainly have preferences and can make choices that are different. As Vatican II was beginning to awaken the Roman church, Wendy Carlos brought the Boomer generation up to date with Columbia Records' 1968 *Switched on Bach*. It took nothing away from the original or the tradition, but just made it bigger and more profound. "Nothing," that is, unless one is more interested in "maintaining the original" rather than "making it flesh." In religious terms, this means we are more interested in "Churchianity" and less in "Christianity."[1]

Just like we don't effectively communicate if we're not speaking the same language, no authentic meaningful living liturgy exists without some degree of inculturation. I can listen to someone speaking a language of which I'm ignorant and can have a guess at what they are trying to tell me, but it's just that, guesswork. If the speaker isn't doing the work of enculturation, the listener must. Or, alternatively, they can just not bother and walk away, which is what happens in churches too.

When culture changed very little for multiple decades, ritual could also remain unchanged, but as times shifted (the printing press, the educated merchant classes, the rise of artisans and professional musicians, through to the industrial revolution and beyond), unchanging ritual began to have its relevance questioned. As culture continues to change at a faster and faster rate, so do the challenges to keep ritual relevant for each generation. The question must be answered over and over: What are we doing and why?

The Reformation tackled the issues that were most prevalent by the early 1500s, but things didn't change universally, nor did the influences for the need for continual change go away. The exodus of the Puritans from England in 1620 aboard the *Mayflower* reminds us that cultural issues didn't end with the Reformation. Even in recent times, while we can easily see the cultural changes of the past hundred years all around, and note the challenges these have created for religion as well as the arts, we need to remember this is not a unique twentieth-century phenomenon brought about by the likes of Karl Marx, Pablo Picasso, Antonin Artaud or Pope John XXIII.

One example that our problems aren't new is the voice of (now Blessed) Antonio Rosmini, a nineteenth-century Italian priest, polymath, and founder of The Institute of Charity (also known as the Rosminians). One of his books, *The Five Wounds of the Church* (originally published in Italy in 1848), dramatically locates the five big problems facing the Roman Catholic church of his time in the wounds of the crucified body of Jesus as thus:

---

1. "Churchianity" is a wonderful word which I came across a few years ago. It's defined in Merriam-Webster as: *a usually excessive or narrowly sectarian attachment to the practices and interests of a particular church.* It was apparently first used in 1837 and is deserving of a new lease on life.

Left hand—the lack of connection and communication between the clergy and the people in the celebration of the mass and other rituals. This is due to . . .

Right hand—the lack of appropriate education and learning among the clergy, with a lack of priority for what is important in their training, especially scripture and evangelization. This is due to . . .

The wound in the side—the disconnect between the people, the clergy, and (as the chief teachers of the diocese), the bishops. This is not helped by . . .

Right Foot—too much interest among the bishops (and clergy) in worldly power and influence, and concerns with money and prestige, which is rooted in . . .

Left foot—the still-practiced feudal system of property ownership and fiefdom in the church, which makes bishops into landlords, not partners in ministry.[2]

Before we celebrate his perceptions and clear articulation of the problem too loudly, we need to remember that Rosmini was poisoned to death by conflicting factions within the Roman church (one could suggest names, or at least a religious group, but proof is lacking), reminding us that our culture wars of today are not the worst they've ever been. Indeed, in the West we've stopped burning each other at the stake too (at least for the moment). However, his story supports the idea that we have been living in a tension between Christianity and Churchianity probably since Constantine, and that tension is not going away on its own anytime soon. This in turn means we must ask the question of any ritual, "is this responding to our cultural lived Christianity, or our structural Churchianity?"

To pretend that a long-standing link between culture and ritual doesn't exist is to forget that the church, just like theater, is a human way of responding to the felt need for "something" that helps us articulate the "otherness" of our humanity which goes beyond what we can see, hear, taste, smell, and touch. As said above, all known ancient native and

---

2. Blessed Rev. Antonio Rosmini IC (1797–1855) was a forward-thinking theologian and philosopher whom Alessandro Manzoni (for whom Verdi wrote his famous *Requiem,*) referred to as "the only contemporary Italian author worth reading." Mingardi, Alberto (2007). *Intro to The Constitution Under Social Justice.* Lexington Books. p. xl. It is said Pope St. John XXIII had a copy of *The Five Wounds* by his bedside throughout the time of the Second Vatican Council. True or not, one can see Rosmini's influence in subsequent contemporary Catholic thought through to the ministry and words of Pope Francis.

aboriginal cultures that gathered ritually also included some sense of the Great Spirit, of gods or demi-gods, named or otherwise, who at different times had to be invoked, engaged, placated, or paid off.

A famous quote often attributed to the nineteenth-century composer Gustav Mahler, though it may be older than him, says: "Tradition is the handing down of the flame, not the worshiping of the ashes."[3] He's also credited with another similar line, aimed at the (solid and traditional) theater of his day, which goes: "What many theater people call tradition is just coziness and laziness." As individuals and communities, we should reflect on our attitude to the traditions and rituals of our life which we treat as immutable, (hidden Churchianity,) and reflect on this challenge, asking which elements have become coziness and lazy rather than life-giving and generative, a truly lived Christianity.

Let us also note that Mahler (if indeed it was he who coined both phrases) compares Tradition (here with a capital T), which is the essence of the reality of something which is immutable and eternal, with our little traditions (here with a small t), which is shorthand for "doing what I think we've always done." I remember being told years ago that "doing anything three consecutive times makes it a tradition." We do have short memories!

A good dramaturge and a good liturgist are always mindful of their respective Traditions and their ability to carry the meaning and power of a production or liturgy, and yet are also aware of the tendency to coziness and laziness which familiarity and lack of reflection can bring. They are equally mindful of not getting caught in any false "ought" by what less experienced minds feel is a tradition, one that isn't actually rooted in the essence of the message and intention of the script or author, but just a manifestation of the "we've always done it that way" energy.

The words of the prophet Isaiah (43:19) come to mind:

> *I am about to do a new thing;*
> *now it springs forth; do you not perceive it?*
> *I will make a way in the wilderness*
> *and rivers in the desert.*

I would suggest God didn't just do a new thing once. No true artist makes a new thing once either. God and artists are always trying to find a

---

3. The online Classical Music Guide Forums has an extensive thread of conversations about the possible source of this quote, but all lack references. Various suggestions include St. Thomas More, Pope St. John XXIII, and Benjamin Franklin. The most popular seems to be philosopher Jean Jaures, a contemporary of Mahler.

new source of insight, a new expression to help people find a contemporary way through the confusion of life, finding new symbols of both the past and the future. This is what every director and production team is doing when they ask the question, "What is our production of this particular script at this particular time and place adding to the world today?" The answer may be as simple as "bringing more joy and laughter," though that's often the hardest thing to do. Whatever else it is, every production is hoping to find the "new" and meaningful for its contemporary audience.

For liturgy, rooted as it is in ritual, the challenge is to keep a firm hold on the essence of the Tradition, but not unconsciously to start from any false "ought" derived from the habits and answers ("little traditions") of more recent or even ancient times and places. One might make the same choices, and that's okay, but we need to do it consciously, with awareness and having looked at all the options we can think of. And this takes work, wisdom, and questioning.

The word which links this work for both stage and altar is "presence," and more particularly "real presence." The end product in both situations is for everyone to experience the "real presence" of something which is (or, in the case of the Divine, someone who is) greater and beyond what actually happened, more than just the words and the actions, the costumes and the lights. That end product is a visceral yet also, usually, indefinable experience of "something" which leaves us with a feeling of joy, sadness, compassion, or gratitude. When it works, it's about really seeing, and really being seen.

My homiletics professor, Rev. Dr. Margie Brown, paraphrased Maya Angelou when she said to the class of our Sunday preaching, "Three days later they may not remember the words you said or wisdom you shared. What they will still remember is how you made them feel while you were speaking." Their experience of our "real presence" (or lack of it), whether as preacher, performer, or presider, will be what lets us know if we've lived into the possibility of the archetype or not.

So what practical help can a dramaturge and a liturgist offer? First, they're there to listen to thoughts and ideas and often help the leaders (director, leader, pastor) flesh out an initial thought before the participants are brought into the rehearsal or preparation time. Another simple answer is that they can ask a child's questions (remember what Jesus said?) when a proposal is being made: "Why?" "Why not?" "What does that mean?" "Why is that person happy when we hear from them?" "Why isn't that person happy when we hear from them?" "Why is that person wearing that?" and the like.

The good dramaturge and liturgist, in response to an answer of "I don't know," "it seemed a good idea at the time," or "that's what it was like last time," will be able to offer some alternatives with reasons why each are more or less appropriate. And therein lies the reason many professionals don't like these functions on their team, because they don't like being questioned, especially if they haven't thought through their reasons. The wise practitioner will ask for wisdom, ideally providing more than one answer, before they make any decisions, giving them choices in the process of creating. Intuition is, of course, part of the "creative gift," but that doesn't preclude knowledge and wisdom as a confirmatory back-up.[4]

An example of how a dramaturge might interact with a company came when I was in an American community theater production of Agatha Christie's *Witness for the Prosecution*, which is very much an English play set in London. The director was telling the two actors playing attorneys in the court scenes to move around and play the space more fully. Two of us native Brits were in the cast and we were able to point out that in the UK, even today, attorneys in a high court are confined to a small dock and lectern for all examinations and cannot move around as they do in America. The director could do with that information as they wished, our set did not have the furniture of the original building, but now at least they knew that they were breaking a rule that was (and still is) current for the original script and the culture if they did indeed have them move. (They didn't.)

Attitudes to liturgists are mixed, largely because these professionals are frequently seen and sometimes experienced as sole arbiters of taste and protocol rather than team players working towards a common goal. Unfortunately, the preparation of liturgy in most Western, especially eucharistic parishes as an open and active team experience is somewhat rare, with such preparation more usually being independent actions of the music minister picking the hymns and anthems, and the altar guild changing the flowers. Everything else is thought to be prescribed by the denominational liturgical books or the exclusive purview of the presiding clergy.

---

4. A dramaturge will sometimes create a "storyboard" for a production to share with the cast, giving examples of newspaper stories and newsreels from the relevant period, outlining social rules and mores which were current then but are not today, along with general stories that were around then. Particularly worth noting, social interaction between the genders and between races has changed a lot in the past hundred years, as have expectations about clothes, hats, etc.

Until recently this had mainly worked (sort of) for hundreds of years, while the people in the pews were told that (a, as before) they would go to hell if they questioned or disobeyed, and (b) they weren't educated enough to be able to argue back. This power also required the people to believe that what was being done was handed down by the Holy Spirit and Tradition, rooted in scripture and required by God. Little to none of this thinking works any more, and certainly won't in the future. That is not to say the overall intention of liturgy has changed; it hasn't. But everything else has, and that matters.

So what is theater gaining by using an experienced dramaturge and worship losing by not learning how to engage a well-trained liturgist?

One of the main realities is that most liturgy is still working from an understanding of worship as something that is asked for by God and is done in some way to please God. While the language of obligation may not be overtly used in denominations other than the Roman Catholic Church, the motivation for "why should we go to church?" has not been clarified beyond (a) the third commandment to "keep holy the sabbath day," (b) it's good for you, and (c) it's how we show we belong. None of these are incorrect, of course. However, the modern reality is that even most folks brought up as churchgoers believe that God doesn't need their worship, even though they may indeed want a relationship with their experience of the Divine. For many, church is best understood as an optional service and community organization for their spiritual and social benefit for when they have time or need it. This latter is particularly important as people age. Church can be a very important social connection and safety net as we age, especially if we're single, even if too many of today's pastors think it's only about getting young families involved. As one Episcopal priest friend commented, "people are not having children the way they used to, but they are all still getting old. So where's the real demographic for market development?"

Even though attendance has declined, many churches promote themselves as service and community organizations and, again, this is not a wrong thing. Christian communities should be filled with the work of the deacons and community members feeding "orphans and widows," bringing folks together and helping members care for one another. The wonderful advert of "see how they love one another" (1 Peter 1:22–23 and Tertullian [c.160–225 CE], *Apologeticus* Ch. 39, sect. 7) hopefully rings true and powerfully. Indeed, the social welfare work of Christian and other faith groups, supported by all people of goodwill across the world, includes food banks, emergency aid, health clinics, schools, and clothing and furniture stores in a great and good publicly affirmed credit to humanity. The need is not going away anytime soon.

So why, with all these great works of love out in the world to advertise faith in action, is attendance dropping calamitously? The list of contributing answers is unfortunately well-known to most of us and not so short. In brief (for it is not the subject of this book), we can list:

- The misuse of social power at a structural level
- Abuse of individuals at a personal level
- An archaic structure and (for some denominations) form of dress which is more attentive to self-preservation in the name of Tradition than contemporary relevance
- Poor presentation of the fundamental message of the gospels
- An equally poor living out of the same, especially involving financial impropriety
- Poor quality and irrelevant church services, especially in preaching (and there we come back to the purpose of this book)

This is not a new list—it's consisted of the same elements for well over a thousand years to different degrees—but now the consequences in terms of church attendance are growing exponentially. While attempting to bring back belief in hell might seem like a good partial solution (Spoiler alert: it's not!), taking a long hard look at what we're doing in our liturgical services might at least have benefits for those of us still attending church and might work to bring others in or back.

Looking at which Christian churches *are* growing in the West (Asia, Africa, and South America are different stories), the statistics point very clearly to megachurches and/or churches with very contemporary services (especially the music), with relaxed, informal, and engaged atmospheres and expectations. A cross may or may not be in the space, but never a crucifix. The space may utilize a more theatrical lighting rig than in a traditional church, with a screen for following the words to songs, and maybe with accompanying images too. No or very few communion Sundays will be offered, and the Common Lectionary will probably not be used. While this model is most frequently seen over the past thirty or forty years in the United States, it can be seen elsewhere too. For example, large-scale Evangelical Pentecostalism is growing in Latin America, even as traditional Roman Catholicism shrinks. The media would also suggest a rather more fundamentalist approach to theology in these growing churches, providing more answers than opportunities to explore questions, very reminiscent of medieval Europe.

Before we get too taken up by attributing their popularity to the significant theatricality of many of these churches and their worship services, we should remember that very little on this planet is more theatrical than a pontifical High Mass in a Roman Catholic or Anglican cathedral. I've seen productions of Puccini's opera *Tosca* which felt like they had fewer candles and supernumeraries! So it's not about theatricality as such. What's different is the level of engagement at an emotional and "feeling" level one can expect in each. One way to look at this is the degree to which each type of service appeals to that which is more introverted in each of us, or more extroverted.

At a very basic statistical level, according to an article in *Psychology Today*, introverts are said to be represented by somewhere between 16 and 50 percent of the population, while extroverts are somewhere between 50 and 74 percent.[5] Even if the actual balance were 50/50, what's true is that each of us has a propensity for being socially engaged on a scale which flows from "I only like to meet people one person at a time, and then no more than three people in a week," to "bring on the all-night party every night!"

As the article points out:

> As it turns out, the brains of introverts and extroverts are wired differently! The front part of introvert's brains is most active and stimulated by solitary activities while the back part of extrovert's brains is most active. This part of the brain is stimulated by sensory events coming in from the external world! In addition, a chemical called "dopamine" is released by our brains whenever we experience something positive. It's an automatic reward center and makes us feel good! Extroverts need more dopamine to feel an effect, whereas introverts have a low dopamine threshold. They don't require a lot of stimulation to feel rewarded.[6]

5. https://www.jibc.ca/sites/default/files/community_social_justice/pdf/cl/Introverts_and_Extroverts_(Psychology_Today).pdf Also: See also https://www.christianity.com/wiki/christian-life/introvert-no-apology-required-11626582.html.

6. Buettner, Dan, Thrive, 14 May 2012 and published in Psychology Today. Online. http://www.psychologytoday.com/collections/201207/introverts-extroverts/are-extroverts-happier-introverts Date of last access 2013-13-24.

When we add this to the fact that, according to a report in the UK from 2021, somewhere around 68 percent of Catholic clergy see themselves as introverted, while only about 25 to 40 percent of non-Catholic clergy are, we can see a source of this difference is style.[7]

Effectively, while extroverted individuals find it "boring" to go to the more "old fashioned" services, introverted folk will feel much more at home, and the clergy there are more likely to also be "in the same vein." Extroverts, on the other hand, will feel at home and "in synch with" the more extroverted clergy and style of the lively and media-focused engaged energy of contemporary megachurches.

Also, when we look at the origins of the different Christian church services, we see early monastic roots showing forth more so at the "Traditional" end of the range (along with most Anglican, Episcopalian and Catholic clergy and parishioners), than at the free-style Evangelical end. Further, the monastic world, which nurtured so much of our liturgical tradition from the fifth century, is even more strongly introverted than the average Catholic clergy population. Hence, we have a liturgical form which was created mainly by introverted monks now being delivered by a clergy population which is significantly in step with such an introverted style, and then we wonder why it doesn't work for the 50 to 74 percent of the population who are extroverts. If those remaining in the "liturgical" pews are mainly introverted, that they don't sing loudly (a myth proved as much by the exceptions as any) is no surprise. Apart from anything else, this all puts enormous pressure on the music and preaching, as this is the only part of the average liturgy which can "break the fourth wall" and directly connect with people.

The balance of extroverts and introverts in a particular population varies across the globe, and across individual countries, urban versus rural, etc. We see here therefore at least one possible reason why some churches have a much better chance of finding their roots and popularity in one particular style as opposed to another when people are presented with choices. We also see why one particular pastor and the team they feel comfortable gathering around themselves (because like tends to gather like) are more or less "at home" in a particular denomination and locality. The purpose for exploring this example of potential conflict and challenge is that this is exactly the type of situation where a good liturgist can help provide wisdom and practical options to help the clergy and

---

7. *Mental Health, Religion and Culture* 25.9 (2022) 884–96 https://doi.org/10.1080/13674676.2021.2017420.

team meet the needs of the people who are different from them. The challenge then, however, would be that the clergy and ministers might need to change, or at least learn a new skillset. This is also where good ongoing personal training can help provide techniques for getting the job done when an easy fit doesn't seem likely, such as among the interestingly high percentage of introverts in the theater.

I do not intend to try to solve the attendance problems of the mainline churches. That will require, I suspect, a new "awakening" and a *lot* of changes. However, I'm hoping that by pointing to where they might find helpful skills and techniques for doing their jobs, clergy will be able to learn to present the liturgy they choose to create in a way where they're comfortable, and which *also* enables more folks in the congregation to connect with and benefit from the celebration on any particular day.

The issue is not, of course, limited to Christianity. It also explains the phrase my Jewish friends use when they move to a new city, "shul shopping."[8]

The introverted prayer leader doesn't have to become extroverted, or vice versa, but they can learn to craft a whole experience, like one does with a play, where the ancillary elements apart from the minister help fill in the gaps, creating a whole experience which no one person can do alone. This mixture becomes a more active team approach. By drawing in someone like a liturgist with knowledge of the textual background, the physical options and the way one can communicate the script, one is not alone. Like a dramaturge, a liturgist's job is not to dictate answers but to provide options and choices, and hopefully direct those interested to further training.

CHOOSING YOUR SCRIPT

Some plays have more than one version. Even written in the same language in which a company will perform it, a version can and does change. Shakespeare, for example, is often edited and/or updated in language. Popular foreign language plays written by the likes of Chekov and Ibsen, very common on Broadway and in London's West End, will often get a new translation if one hasn't been done in a while. And though something might almost always be "lost in translation," something is always

---

8. https://religionnews.com/2023/03/29/shul-shopping-in-new-york-a-jewish-millennials-two-years-of-wandering.

gained, which is that the main elements of the script can be understood by a contemporary audience of a different cultural group.

Just as a good dramaturge can help a director or company chose the best translation of a play, including the original, so a good liturgist can help a church community understand how language (including music and environmental arts) works to further or hinder the aims of the liturgy for a parish. This work starts with an understanding of the permitted texts for a denomination, or any outlines that must be followed for communities not limited by specific prayer books. These books aren't just found at the liturgical end of the worship spectrum, including Catholic or Orthodox churches, the Anglican and Episcopal communion, along with many Lutherans and Presbyterians, but also with many Reformed churches. Only unaffiliated churches, such as "Community" or "Free" churches, are regularly without official guidelines, if not also requirements.

These prayer books and sacramentaries are full of liturgical direction and acceptable theological concepts (carefully written to avoid known heresies), directed towards helping us be philosophically orthodox. By using these over and over the teacher-within-the-writer hopes to form the minds and therefore actions of the congregation to be good Christians in the world. And by "good" they mean not just right-acting (orthopraxy) but also right-thinking (orthodoxy) and not heretical. To be clear once again, these are not bad aims. We hear maybe thousands of words every service, hundreds of millions of words over a lifetime, all ultimately directed at forming the hearts and minds of the congregation by letting them eavesdrop on the conversation the presider has with God. A priest's prayers aren't likely to change God, but they're very clearly crafted with the intention of changing us.

However, I don't believe these are the prayers which move and transform. Certainly, no author I know of would expect to get a play published or performed if all they did was fill the time with logical arguments and didactic interchanges. The great Irish writer George Bernard Shaw[9] was a magnificent talent in getting an audience to agree with the two opposite sides of an argument at the same time, but he did it with skill and humor and still engaged the emotions and imagination. In the hands of a lesser talent these storylines would be boring and never performed. Unfortunately, most liturgical scripts are written by theologians and ritual

---

9. If you wish to see some examples of Shaw's great skill at writing two sides of the same argument and leaving the audience in the middle, try *The Apple Cart* or *Man and Superman*.

theorists, not by skilled writers. That's not to say attempts haven't been made to expand the options.

For example, in 1984 the International Committee on English in the Liturgy proposed to Rome what became known in the UK as Eucharistic Prayer A for discussion within the Roman Catholic Church.[10] Following the traditional form for such prayers, biblical images were used (this time including feminine ones), as well as more poetic language than was used in older versions in leading the congregation through the various prescribed parts of the prayer (doxology, epiclesis, institution narrative, anamnesis, etc.). Eucharistic Prayer A was rejected by the Roman authorities of the day because, according to the grapevine, (no official reason is ever given,) it was considered not theological enough. To this day it's still a favorite prayer for many for exactly that reason. It fulfills the purpose of the prayer (giving thanks to God, etc.), while at the same time creating an inviting narrative which engages the imagination, not just the mind, and to which the congregation can say an enthusiastic "Amen!" In a world where presiders have choices about which prayers they use, it's important to look at the material and judge for yourself (if you are willing to take the risk), if it'll work for your specific congregation. A good liturgist can help with this. Just as all our Bible readings are only used in translation and even cultural adaptation, so too do the major prayers come with a lot of theological justification, (or baggage, depending on one's view,) which might have made sense historically and certainly do theologically, but could be questioned on the grounds of if they help us pray in the here and now. From a cultural point of view, this eucharistic prayer was written in English, for use in countries which speak English, and was not a translation of an Italian or Latin original. One wonders how many native English speakers were on the review body in Rome.

For those who are interested, the link for ICEL's *An Original Eucharistic* Prayer (see note below) also gives (8–10) the Anglican text for what they adapted and then published as Eucharistic Prayer G in *Common Worship* in 2000, 201–3. This is a good opportunity to compare and contrast how different churches use language and rubrics in a unique way for their respective communions.

Having said all that, I know some Catholic communities love the Latin Mass, (I did too as a teenager,) and I've worked with traditional

---

10. ICEL An Original Eucharistic Prayer: Text 1 1984. https://drive.google.com/file/d/0BxZeTtRK3_J5dTZSRos3dHBqbHM/view?resourcekey=0-NiaoP4yGp-MxVhsJqIOVeg.

Episcopal communities who love the language of Rite 1, even though it's hardly been updated from its seventeenth-century origins and theology. When working for them, I would never dream of changing a word, and the same would be true of other traditionalist communities in any tradition. However, I wouldn't be in favor of using such prayers for a general congregation on a regular basis, especially one without a firm history in the tradition, which in most contemporary cases is almost no one. A presider, like any public speaker, needs to know their audience. That is part of being a pastor, not just a minister. Choose your script wisely! Read and study the options. And, where necessary, consider making "cultural adaptations" to fit your congregation's time and place. (And yes, I said the focus of the choice is what will work for the congregation, not just what the presider prefers.) Again, this is the world in which a good liturgist will be comfortable and helpful.

Added to this, the option is always provided to keep historical texts the same but to set them in more contemporary ways. Many composers have done this very successfully. Sometimes singing a sentiment can be much more acceptable than hearing someone say it.

Worth remembering is that many churches have liturgical options available for services with children and youth which are rarely used on Sundays, which is a shame. After all, most adults still have a child-like theology, and are we not all "children of God"? Know all your potential scripts and focus on the intention of the work: helping the people to pray. If the language and simplicity of childhood helps everyone pray, maybe a simpler liturgy is a good choice

The purpose for encouraging this reflection at the local level is based on the quality of the material and whether it's "fit for purpose" as a script for communicating what the ritual is intended to communicate. Most people in the pews aren't interested in a theology lesson on Sunday. (I doubt God is either.) What they are interested in is being helped to pray, being inspired, feeling more deeply the unending love of God which *always* offers understanding, encouragement and, when necessary, forgiveness.

For this reason I believe the quote from *Environment and Art* is so important. We have to remember that the purpose of liturgy is to enable the people to pray and experience the Divine. God doesn't need reminding or helping; we do. A good liturgist understands this primary function and helps a team to direct everything to this end.

We use far too many words on a Sunday. If we must use so many, let each count as much as any good author and cast works to ensure they do when creating a play. God and God's people deserve nothing less.

If anyone needs further motivation for doing this work, I refer them to the oft-quoted wise words of Abraham Joshua Herschel:

It is customary to blame secular science and anti-religious philosophy for the eclipse of religion in modern society. It would be more honest to blame religion for its own defeats. Religion declined not because it was refuted, but because it became irrelevant, dull, oppressive, insipid. When faith is completely replaced by creed, worship by discipline, love by habit; when the crisis of today is ignored because of the splendor of the past; when faith becomes an heirloom rather than a living fountain; when religion speaks only in the name of authority rather than with the voice of compassion—its message becomes meaningless.[11]

QUESTIONS TO CONSIDER

1. Do I only ever create liturgies where I'm comfortable? What about the people who are "different from me" in the congregation?

2. How comfortable am I when challenged for my liturgical or preaching choices? Can I listen to other voices?

3. Do I see myself as part of a team united in delivering the script, or do I consider my words and actions more important than those of anyone else?

4. As an author and preacher, do I invite participation from others in my process? How might I build a team or work more collaboratively with colleagues and peers?

---

11. From *God in Search of Man: A Philosophy of Judaism*.

5

Communication, Relationship, Change

The Theory and Consequence of How Words Have Meaning Between People

The script is not the play; the prayers are not the liturgy.

MANY DECADES AGO, I read a book called *She and Me* by E. Graham Howe (d.1975). Howe was an early British follower of Freud's psychoanalysis, though known for his lack of technical jargon. He also included an openness to spirituality and alternative theories in his work, which links him closely with Carl Jung.[1] In his attempt to help people understand his thinking, this book begins with a rather large glossary. Howe carefully defines each word he'll be using that might have any confusing meaning, as well as linking words he considers intimately connected. One group of definitions has stayed with me ever since. They are:

---

1. Howe is an interesting though overlooked source for exploring the meaning within liturgy and in healing. For those interested, William Stranger edited *The Druid of Harley Street—The Spiritual Psychology of E. Graham Howe*. (Harley Street, in London, is famous for housing the consulting rooms for the UK's leading medical and psychological practitioners.)

Communication—the exterior, expressed experience of meeting (see Relationship).
Relationship—the interior, unexpressed experience of meeting (see Suffering).
Suffering—the experience of change.

We need to start at the end of this trinity and address what Howe meant by an experience of suffering as being an experience of change. For Howe (and others in his field), any change requires us to go through an experience of letting go of our old synthesis or paradigm on which we are basing all or part of our daily life to make room for some new reality. (For "letting go" one can also read "experience a death and bereavement.") Every change is a little death. That new fact might be quite insignificant in the big scheme of things, such as, "Wow, turns out curry *isn't* necessarily going to burn my mouth and stomach!" Integrating this new fact, however, opens us up to new vistas of dining and requires us to apologize to our past culinary self for having denied ourselves the joy of eating curry based on a false truth.

Similarly, while we don't normally equate realizing in adulthood that green beans are actually quite edible with the experience of other deaths and bereavements in our life, the realization does require us, ever so minimally, to accept that our past four-year-old self was inappropriately judgmental and that we owe probably several people (parents, grandparents, school cooks) an apology for our accusations that they were trying to poison us.

As people change, even positive changes we've been working on for some time (such as giving up an addiction) requires us in some way to admit "I was wrong; I was making excuses for myself that weren't based in truth or honesty." And while there may be a physical dimension to that suffering (such as the aches and pains after starting to go to the gym again), a parallel internal psychological change also affects how I understand myself and consequentially my relationship to everything and everyone else around me.

Change is an essential part of two distinct processes which are at the root and center of why we traditionally do theater and church. We are seeking revelation to bring about a catharsis (healing) and metanoia (change of direction), a turning around of our focus and spirit, admitting we were headed in the wrong direction and the motivation to point our feet in a new way. Without a real change (a "little death," a true apology), no matter how small, no catharsis or healing occurs, and similarly no metanoia, no turning around. This little death causes us to effect a change in our viewpoint and direction of action. Having said that, and now knowing where we're heading, let's go back to Howe's sequence of definitions.

Howe defines communication, a hugely popular word today, as the external dimension of what most people mean when they use the word, such as shaking hands with someone and introducing themselves, or writing an email or social media post. For Howe, just because someone has done an act of communication doesn't mean the other person has received it. This is a simple but critical point. I may send you a text, which is a form of communication, but until you've read it, we haven't started the process which (we hope) will lead to connection. To do that, Howe suggests, requires a second state either to exist already or to begin; namely, we need to have a relationship. Not only that, the internal degree or depth of our relationship will determine the degree or depth of our communication. The message "Meet me tonight to get what you deserve" might be delightful to receive if you're someone who wants to use my in-store discount to buy an expensive item, but could be seen as threatening to someone who knows me only peripherally.

The classic example is to think of how many times we have said (and hopefully will continue to say) "I love you." We use the same sentence to express our connection to our significant others, our pets, our parents, and our favorite foods. Hopefully we mean something different in each of these situations. (If you truly love bacon as much as your spouse, you probably need to get help.) Every time we say "I love you" we're qualifying the words based on the relationship. You might be willing to die for a spouse or a child, but hopefully not for a piece of your favorite cheesecake, even if you did just say "I'm dying to try that new flavor." Indeed, most users of English are technically proficient enough to be able to use the same words for opposite effect, such as how the words "yeah, sure, right" can mean both "I totally agree" and "you're completely wrong and an idiot." Clever, huh?

The meaning of words changes based not just on relationship but also context and delivery. They're only good in getting our information across as far as we can both hear the inflection in the voice (which is difficult with written words), as well as understand the relationship between the words that are spoken or written. And yet they're all we have when we read a script for either a play or an act of worship. This is why a script (theatrical or liturgical) is not and will never be an experience of a play or an act of worship. In the theater and in church, words need a body and breath in time and space to become communication.

What Howe's definitions explain to us is that we use external means to communicate, but that those words only take on their meaning in the moment they're spoken, based on the relationship between the speaker and the listener. What's more (and here's the crunch), they'll only do the work for which we uttered them if both the speaker and the listener are open to be changed by them, even if that change involves suffering.

Or, to look at it from the other direction: If I'm not willing to be changed by communication within a relationship, then I'm not actually in a real relationship. And if we're not in a relationship, then my words will lack ultimate meaning, for they have nowhere to land, no environment or context within which to be heard.[2]

If one were to try to put this wisdom into one sentence, equally applicable to the work of actors, presiders, and preachers, it might be: "If you've never been changed by the words you speak, then you've never found the best way to say them, and never communicated the fullest depths of meaning that are in those words". That might seem a little harsh, but it points to the challenge of the job. We can't expect others to be open to being changed by what we say if we're not open to it ourselves. Not necessarily in the same way, to the same degree, to the same result, but openness to change (or sometimes we might say "to be moved") seems essential for the successful fulfillment of the tasks at hand.

Some colleagues in other professions speak of their continual need to do the exact opposite, to stay separate from their work or otherwise be emotionally "eaten alive" by the suffering, the failure and the raw feelings. Teachers, nurses, doctors, and social workers talk of it often. Police officers and armed service members bring it up in therapy (it's too hard to mention it in their workplaces). I know lawyers, despite all the jokes to the contrary, who (at least figuratively) sometimes cry themselves to sleep at night because of their relationship to their work for the poor and disadvantaged. And then we wonder why alcohol, smoking, and other addictions, as well as burnout and even suicide are too common in these professions.

---

2. I have known many people in relationships over the decades, and too many have been with partners who were never likely to be open to changing. Regardless of whether it's familial, spousal, or fraternal, a lack of openness to being changed by the relationship limits the depth of communication that can happen within it. I can rarely ask another person to change if I am not willing to change too.

We might use the phrase "being authentic" to describe when we feel someone is aware of the challenge of change implied in what they have to say. There's a vulnerability in the exchange, even though the news may have more consequences for the one receiving it than the one giving it. This experience might also include a sense of empathy for the one who will be most impacted, which is of course a very real component of being in a relationship with someone. Examples might be telling someone they've lost their job, or failed a test, or are pregnant. The classic "this will hurt me more than it will hurt you" is a good example of the opposite!

If those who carry the archetypes of performers and ministers (ordained or not) aren't able to model how to carry and work through this challenge of being human, how can we reasonably expect others to be able to do so? Our scripts, for both stage and church, are full of these challenges. The canon of stories both groups tell are rife with the consequences of not living in truth, not living in the present moment, not being open to forgiveness, not offering forgiveness, fearing death and whatever is next, and we've been telling these stories for as long as both professions have existed.

One of the miracles of the later twentieth and twenty-first centuries is that professionals across the performing arts (acting as cultural priests very much in the tradition of Artaud and others) have stepped in to fill the gap left by those churches which haven't been open to the present moment and its ongoing challenges and changes. Society began to apply words like "equality," "inclusion," and "justice" to women for the first time only in the last hundred or so years, and some churches still aren't on board. One of the common arguments back in the day was that "the people aren't ready for it." In other words, potential change and suffering wasn't a price the leadership was willing to pay to have an honest conversation about their relationship with that half of humanity. We can then add the well-known other contemporary issues of racial inclusion, along with gender and sexual diversity, which different churches have avoided or embraced at different times. Interestingly, the creative arts have largely embraced these supposed challenges if for no other reason than representatives of these groups "just started doing it" and didn't wait for any official affirmation or permission. This is the freedom individuals and groups have when they're comfortable living on the periphery of society and any power structure. The closer one is to the center, the harder it is to change.

If historically a performing company didn't employ people of color or women, then the people of color or women formed their own performing company. In this twenty-first century of ours, the performing and other arts have a significant number of women, people of color, homosexuals and transgender persons in their official ranks, and most of the churches still find it difficult to talk about these subjects, even though these people are in their pews. Interestingly, American black churches have been proficient at "doing their own thing" on the racial issue since the time of slavery, though elsewhere in the Western white world growth and integration has been much slower.[3] In the latter twentieth century the development of churches like Roman Catholic Women Priests and the Metropolitan Community Church are examples on the church side of people who've taken the "just do it" approach, though integration and respect from mainline denominations has been slow.

Viewing history through the lens of Howe's definitions, what was happening here? When an organization wasn't open to change, they weren't able to sustain their relationship with certain other groups. Consequentially, they ceased to be in any form of effective communication with them. The two sides couldn't "hear" each other. We see this over and over in contemporary society. We say people have stopped listening to one another, and we are correct. Why? Because each side no longer has any interest in changing, be it MAGA or progressive, pro-choice or pro-life, a Latin-mass goer or a supporter of Pope Francis. Where no openness to change exists, including the potential need to admit one was wrong (or at least able to shift their opinion about something), no relationship exists, and hence no effective communication.

Cynicism and soapboxes aside, one of the reasons that preachers and presiders of worship can learn a lot from the practitioners of the performing arts is precisely this modeling of how the latter have accepted the challenge to engage with difficult topics, sometimes by placing opposing views on stage together. To coin a phrase, "Theater doesn't avoid drama, indeed, it thrives on it." Alternatively, for many churches, conflict avoidance is a powerful force in the face of difficult conversations.

---

3. As an example, *Fire in the Pews* is an excellent documentary produced by the African American Bishops of the Roman Catholic Church in the US about being Black and Catholic. It's a great example of enculturation and taking ownership of the rites. The title comes from one of the priests who comments "you can't have fire in the pews while you've got ice in the pulpit." It'd be interesting to see companion pieces from other churches and representing other groups, even one representing the "majority" too. What would a documentary video about being white and Methodist, or Latinx and Lutheran cover and express culturally?

PEOPLE NEED TO SEE THEMSELVES IN THE STORY

One of the comments one will frequently hear in listening to different individuals of all backgrounds is that "I didn't know people like me could do that/be that until I saw . . ." This applied historically to, for example, short people in the military, women as doctors, persons with autism as actors, or blind people as professional singers as much as it did to people of color as professional ballet dancers and women as ministers. Many still struggle just to be considered a possibility in some situations. At every step of those individual journeys people fell into one of three camps, effectively saying either: "You're right, you can do that, go for it!", "I've never seen someone like you do that—is it allowed?", or "That's just wrong—people like you shouldn't do that."

Every person who has broken through a glass (or more opaque and even law-enforced) barrier has had to suffer and fight for their place in the world, their profession, and the right to follow their calling. All these pioneers suffered on their journey to bring about change. From this suffering comes the authenticity of the story they're trying to communicate. (And, in authenticity, is the root of that word "author" again!) This suffering is commonly the topic of theater, and the same criteria can also be applied to many of the stories of scripture. While we commonly say that theater is based on the drama of conflict, we might be more correct to say that theater is based on the challenges of human change. These stories, and the positive outcomes that can happen because of them, are what we're trying to communicate both on the stage and in the sanctuary.

Each culture and community tells the story about "who we are" and "how we are" in the world. The stories normalize though sometimes also sanitize and editorialize what's acceptable and therefore what should be considered achievable or not. Those who won't follow the rules implied in these stories are, to varying degrees, shut out or even thrown out of the power and status of the tribe. The words "troublemaker," "deviant" and even "evil" get used frequently. Our human communal attachment to the status quo of "normality" is remarkably strong, along with the apparent need to choose scapegoats from these "abnormal" groups to blame when things go wrong.

One could argue that social barriers protecting supposed "normality" haven't been greatly missed once they've been breached and the space allowed to grow green again. While, for example, some people still think a woman's place is only in the home, most people don't. While not every woman who has taken her place in the world has been without fault, the percentages are, I suspect, no worse than those for the men who have misused their status and power for ill. And men have been doing that for a lot longer. Women, more to the point, are becoming more vocal about the higher standards to which they are held, and many minorities say the same.

The minority of straight, white, males who fear this truth are rising up on social media and elsewhere, raging against the perceived dying of their imagined light. Their bereavement anger is real, and not the easiest place to start a conversation about the truth. Yet most others hope Dr. King's arc of moral justice continues to bend heavenward, and for that we need to have conversations based on building real relationships which can be fruitful with change.

If you wish to see an example of Howe's trinity of process being successful (against the odds,) in practice, read or go see the play *Oslo* by J. T. Rogers, which recounts the previously secret back-channel negotiations which resulted in the Oslo Peace Accord. Rogers later (2021) adapted it for a powerful movie of the same name.

When we explore historical individuals and societies which were more concerned about conserving their "look, feel, and traditions" than exploring an openness to change, we find societies more attuned to control, sometimes by violent means of enforcing it. Tradition with a capital "T," and rules over its manifestations, is preferred over a living tradition open to evolution. The more change is feared, the more relationships tend to be carefully prescribed so that change is avoided, which in turns limits communication to perfunctory roles. One thinks of the external social norms and image of Victorian England, which hid a miasma of decay and violence. Truth, as anyone who is paying attention knows, is still sacrificed in the name of appearances even in the twenty-first century.

While societies continue to be in flux as they seek the new balances required to accommodate change (for each culture may find a different, unique way forward), people seem to vacillate between looking forward to finding that new balance, and backwards to "the good old days." We see this reality mirrored extensively in the performing arts, where the new stories told to affirm these movements towards working out a new, more inclusive normal are present, but where tickets sell best for well-known stories with culturally acceptable endings.

The "new" media platforms since 2000 now give everyone, but especially young people, a chance to see themselves, or at least options for themselves, reflected on their smart phone and TV screens, in videos and movies, and by so-called "influencers". This is important because we humans are mimics at our core, for good and for ill. The stories we tell are ways in which we play with being ourselves. Characters we see and who, thanks to modern technology, even live within our homes become potential models with whom we can identify and relate. The corollary of this is, of course, that there is a significant responsibility for arts and "content" producers to be fully aware that they are creating these "potential futures" for the searching members of society to mirror. Neither church nor stage should step away from the powerful moral imperative to envision a world where truth, justice, and beauty are more attractive than lies, crime, and ugliness, or so most of us would like to believe. Unfortunately, that's rarely where the money is!

A good example of the arts showing society what is possible was in the late 1990s when Gillian Anderson created the character of Dr. Dana Scully in *The X-Files* on TV. The number of girls and young women taking STEM courses at high school and university increased measurably.[4] The magnificent 2016 movie *Hidden Figures* (among others) then followed up this vein with the story of the team of African American women mathematicians who worked at NASA during the early years of the American space program and launch. Truth brings us the possibility of growth, which always requires change. And growth always involves growing pains, the suffering needed for change.

When we see people make the work of creation flesh in their lives, sometimes through fictional stories, sometimes based on fact, we have the possibility to believe we might be able to do it too, sharing a particular charism, viewpoint, or gift. In this way the commitment of a team of creatives (including writers, makeup artists, set and costume designers, as well as directors, producers, and actors) to creating words and being in relationship to those words for all to see suggests the possibility for choices, and therefore change, in others. This work is, at root, a true vocation. It is a living partnership with the Divine in the on-going work of Creation.[5]

---

4. https://www.globalcitizen.org/en/content/xfiles-dana-scully-effect-women-stem/.

5. Support for this view comes from, among others, Karl Rahner, SJ. See his *Karl Rahner's Writings on Literature, Music and the Visual Arts*, translated by Gesa E. Thiessen, published by Bloomsbury

THE CHALLENGE OF EMBRACING CHANGE FOR AN "UNCHANGING" TRADITION

Exploring change is a great challenge for those involved with liturgy, particularly for the preacher and (when not leading liturgy) minister in the role of counselor. People usually only change when they feel safe or have no other choice. Jesus was apparently very good at being present to people and, through building individual relationships, being able to invite them to create change in their own lives. He used what we identified as the essential trinity of gifts needed: Intention, a spoken message (often crafted, we presume, in the moment), and having a body with breath in the present too. However, even with Jesus, it didn't always work. For example, one thinks of most of his interactions with the religious leadership of his day as well as the story of the rich young man (Mk 10:17–22, Mt 19:16–30, Lk 18:18–30).

Presiders often have the limitation of working from a prescribed script, making that personal invitation at least one step removed. Unless a liturgical script invites us to change, the presider can do little to support such action, apart from of course unilaterally changing it.

For the preacher, because they have full control of their script, the decision must be made not if but how to invite those listening to make an even incremental change in one way or another. Howe's trinity of steps (communication, relationship, change) and the Jesus model point the way.

Interestingly, the gospels tell their story by reversing Howe's sequence of definitions. Jesus comes to bring about a new way of living, a change in individual people. He does that by finding ways to establish relationships with them, and into that relationship he speaks what he calls the words of life, sharing a message that is like a refreshing spring flowing inside them that will never dry up.

He does this even when being in relationship with someone will bring about a change in his own status in the community, (an outcast woman at a well, a leper on the highway, a tax collector up a tree, touching the dead,) even to the point of being declared ritually unclean and outside of salvation. He doesn't ask anyone to change their reality until he's done so himself in order to be in a relationship with them, making his words, his communication, more authentic as a result. Individuals and communities of holy men and women have copied this model throughout history, choosing first and foremost to "be" with people rather than to "convert" them. This is what Pope Francis meant when he spoke of the minister needing to "smell like the sheep." The preacher who can work from inside the community, by being in relationship with the people, will always be more powerful in delivering their message than one who remains aloof and outside. The most essential quality of a successful preacher, therefore, is humility, a word which shares its root with humus, "of the earth."

This reality opens us to Howe's wisdom, and to the idea that this is the criteria against which any job which purports to "make the words flesh" should be judged. The problem is that, while theater has often wanted to do something along these lines and has been more and more open to adapting its format to help achieve that end (through such people as the aforementioned Antonin Artaud and Peter Brook, along with Bertolt Brecht, to name a few), worship in the liturgical churches has been hampered by their rigid commitment to certain traditions in this regard. Not, as we said before, that tradition is bad, but it's not the only way. The paradigm of the twenty-first century is more about both-and, not either-or.

Interestingly, some of the theologians and ministers of the more rigorous liturgical churches (which are more introverted in style) have broken new ground (at least theoretically) in their fields of work, creating such approaches as Process, Feminist, and Liberation Theology as alternatives to the historical Substitutional Atonement Theology for interpreting scripture and forming theology. In this way they've opened new ways to enable the integration of all people, socially and religiously, to come about in a way that is not based solely on the premise that "we are all first and foremost sinners." For example, work around what's called Catholic Social Teaching is a systematic call to economic and power equality in the world based on biblical justice, not charity by the rich to the poor.[6]

The non-liturgical churches, on the other hand, have opened themselves to whatever freedom of form they need to communicate the message in their worship, which tends to be more extroverted in style. Interestingly, they've chosen to stick with rather more traditional and sometimes uncritical Substitutional Atonement Theology when confronting human integration and development. The liturgical churches would say that biblical fundamentalism attempts to seal God's self-revelation in an understanding inconsistent with two thousand years of lived history, and that it hampers a living relationship with a God of today. They express

---

6. Catholic Social Teaching is based on seven equal and indispensable principles. https://www.catholiceducation.org/en/religion-and-philosophy/social-justice/seven-principles-of-catholic-social-teaching.html.

this well when, like the Episcopal Church, they say, "We believe scripture is the Word of God, but not necessarily the words of God."

So here we have the conundrum that the "old" churches are outwardly more traditional and introverted but can be intellectually more diverse, whereas the "modern" churches are outwardly more extroverted but inwardly more traditional. Comparing these two approaches, it seems churches are either willing to develop tradition significantly in either liturgical format or theology, but rarely in both at the same time. I've known individuals who embody this conflict, balancing a decidedly progressive theological voice in the pulpit but a traditional, conserving nature at the altar. It can work, but not always comfortably for the congregation.

One could use the old adage of "You pays your money and you takes your choice" when it comes to choosing between these two options. However, one could strongly suggest that the reason nearly all the Western churches are seeing a decline in membership is the fact that people today (younger, possibly more extroverted, often more "change oriented,") are looking for a combination rarely being offered. That combination is both embodied liturgies (and here we're not talking about "swinging from the rafters," but certainly with more outward energy than the average Catholic, Episcopal, or Presbyterian Sunday service,) along with a theological diversity that is strongly rooted in scripture but allows for God's continuing self-revelation to be included and processed.

The same is true of the theater too, of course. Post-COVID theaters are, two to three years later, still challenged to get their audiences back in their seats. Programming, even when production quality is assured, continues to be a big issue. Well-loved shows are more likely to sell out than new ones. Comedies and musicals will outsell dramas and classical works. Asking an audience to think will always be outsold by giving them a laugh and a tune they can whistle on the way home. Famous names will always help, even if they aren't as good as other, less well-known actors. And of course, the price of admission will be a barrier to many, especially during periods of inflation and effective falling wages. What does this tell us?

Put simply, it says that, in both fields, we can go for authenticity and development, or we can go for financial stability, but we're unlikely to get both at the same time. However, we need both to create sustainable communities. And we can find help in an unlikely place.

In my first job out of university I worked for the Philharmonia Orchestra, one of the big four London orchestras, and I remember the manager effectively saying, "We have to balance the season's and each evening's programming with a little of what's good for them and a lot of what our audience likes." Part of my job was that we needed to get commercial sponsorship for those programs which were more around "what's good for them." Not every new (or "new to them") work was enthusiastically received; but because of the quality of the playing and the reputation of the orchestra (developed over time), audiences would usually at least be open to trying "the new," and were surprised when they liked it, which was surprisingly often, I'm glad to say.

Years later when I worked at St. Paschal Baylon Parish in Oakland, California under the excellent Fr. Robert Rein, he used to tell the congregation that we'd challenge them in Lent and Advent but promised them that the Easter and Christmas Seasons would be everything they expected. This "community contract" worked because it developed an openness to the risk of being "met" by a living experience of the Divine and not just fulfilling their Sunday obligation. Fr. Robert had worked for several years to build enough trust within the community to do this and then, with the subsequent positive financial support of the parishioners, invited others of us to come in and work with him to move the work forward.

To draw a parallel and inspiration from an unlikely source, you may remember from your early high school physics the aptly named Law of Inertia. A reminder comes from the Encyclopedia Britannica:

> *Newton's first law (of motion) states that if a body is at rest or moving at a constant speed in a straight line, it will remain at rest or keep moving in a straight line at constant speed unless it is acted upon by a force. In classical Newtonian mechanics, there is no important distinction between rest and uniform motion in a straight line; they may be regarded as the same state of motion seen by different observers, one moving at the same velocity as the particle and the other moving at constant velocity with respect to the particle. This postulate is known as the law of inertia.*[7]

Without external forces, without something or someone believing that "there is more" and bringing energy from outside the system, everything remains in a state of stasis or inertia, or what we commonly call the "status quo." Biologically, stasis and inertia are one (small) step removed from death. The communal function of both dedicated artists and those

---

7. The law of inertia was first formulated by Galileo Galilei for horizontal motion on Earth and was later generalized by René Descartes. https://www.britannica.com/science/Newtons-laws-of-motion.

who truly carry the archetype of preacher and presider is to be the energy that helps humanity not fall into inextricable inertia, stasis, and death.

For the religious side, Richard Rohr OFM states the issue well when he says:

> I believe that religion's unique and necessary function is to lead us into liminal space. Instead, religion has largely become a confirmation of the status quo and business as usual. Religion should lead us into sacred space where deconstruction of the old "normal" can occur. Much of my criticism of religion comes about when I see it not only affirming the system of normalcy but teaching folks how to live there comfortably.[8]

Rohr's "comfortably" and Mahler's "coziness" are the same place.

Jesus did not come primarily to change our minds about God but to change both our experience of God and of our self-understanding (as adopted children), thereby changing our behavior with each other as a way of honoring our Creator.

When Howe gives us his three-step not just definition but requirement for communication, we're challenged by the reality that we might communicate very little because we're scared of being in relationship with each other. We're scared because we're rarely open to being changed by the experience of meeting one other. Yet without that willingness to change we are one step from death, creating a culture of societal stasis based on the fear of change and being converted or transformed. We do this because we're afraid of the suffering that comes with the letting go of our attachments, as Buddhist wisdom teaches us. Dear old Heraclitus, back in 500 BCE Greece, famously said, "The only constant is change," and humanity has been fighting that truth ever since.

True artists, presiders, and preachers attempt to live in a place of unattachment so that they can more easily be open to change. That's their spiritual discipline and the source of their gift to society. Unattachment is not an easy place to be, because it's neither comfortable nor cozy. That's why they need to find support in like-minded communities and can help sustain each other. And that's why society needs to learn to support these communities, because without them doing their hard work we die a slow, change-fearing death.

We'll leave the final words on this subject to Rohr:

---

8. CAC Daily Meditation. 9/26/23 [1] Adapted from Richard Rohr, *Everything Belongs: The Gift of Contemplative Prayer*, rev. ed. (New York: Crossroad Publishing, 2003), 155–56.

I think people who live their lives open to awe and wonder have a much greater chance of meeting the Holy than someone who just goes to church but doesn't live in an open way. We almost domesticate the Holy by making it so commonplace. That's what I fear happens with the way we ritualize worship. I see people come to church day after day unprepared for anything new or different. Even if something new or different happens, they fit it into their old boxes. Their stance seems to be, "I will not be awestruck." I don't think we get very far with that kind of resistance to the new, the Real, and the amazing.[9]

QUESTIONS FOR REFLECTION

1. What have been some of the major moments of change in your life? What did they teach you? How do they help you in your ministry?

2. If you fear change, on what is it based? If you don't ever fear change, why are you so fearless?

3. What does meeting Jesus each day do to you? How do you share that?

4. How do your relationships change the way you do ministry? Can one do ministry if one has never loved?

---

9. Daily Meditation CAC—Richard Rohr OFM. 12/3/2023.

6

Words in my Body
Breath, Movement, Silence and Stillness

The Word was made Flesh and lived among us; it wasn't a concept idea for a discussion group.

To do the work of a performer or liturgical minister without a body is impossible. This might seem an obvious point to make, but given the amount of attention having a body doesn't get in the training of most clergy and other church leaders, you'd think it was an optional extra. A lot of the training that does happen these days is about how to contain the body and be appropriate, especially sexually. This is necessary work, of course. However, this leaves the teaching of Christian leadership, which has an historically uncomfortable relationship with the topic of sex and gender, in a difficult situation. Actors, of course, even voiceover ones who are never seen, are trained from the very beginning to work with their body as a part of their toolbox for manifesting the script. Google a YouTube video of anyone recording an animated movie script (I personally love watching Robin Williams), and the video is an absolute delight.[1]

When speakers forget that their voice begins with their breath, and that breath comes from deep within them, requiring their lungs to inflate and ribs to move, not to mention lips, tongue and throat to be engaged,

1. https://www.youtube.com/watch?v=gwEKZbmrcQw.

then the result is less than optimal. When people get nervous this awareness disappears completely, and the result is often inaudible and sometimes embarrassing.

Here's a simple exercise to show the effectiveness of deep breathing if someone is uncomfortable speaking in public. Stand and say your name and age: "Hello, my name is _____ and I am __ years old." Then relax your knees a little and take three sets of three slow breaths, in for four beats and out for four, first visualizing the air coming into the chest and then out, then the abdomen, and finally the hips. Then say the same sentence again. Almost invariably your voice will be significantly lower, more rounded, and more projected this second time. And you'll feel more confident, as if by magic! But it isn't really magic; it's body science. And even if you don't feel super-confident, with that voice you can "fake it until you make it." That's always a valid *modus operandi* in this regard.

Having mentioned the sex and gender topic, addressing that up front is necessary. Simply put, Christianity (and indeed, most world religions) has never really gotten a handle on sexuality and gender as part of incarnation. Pretending, as some do, that sex is only ever meant to happen during the procreation process is a nice idea, but not one based on any discernable facts or history. The topic seems to remain a significant barrier for many contemporary people to take Christianity seriously, because any discussion of sexuality is still treated as if we were living in Victorian times or even the Middle Ages. If Christianity isn't relevant for today, it's of no use to most people.

While this isn't the place to explore this topic in depth, we're going to assume that the discussion is happening fruitfully elsewhere, and that the outcome will be that we should at least not let the fact that every body is a sexual body detract us from giving the body its significant place in making words flesh. Also, insofar as "making words flesh" is also almost always modeled as being generative in scripture and liturgy, we should assume a generative dimension to all human enfleshed communication and relationships, and that change also always has a creative dimension.

Allow me to justify this line of thought briefly: The Jewish creation story in the Book of Genesis is unique in terms of ancient texts in that the universe is created by speech and not by gods having sex or playing in the mud. This then translates to the Christian idea of words being necessary to effect (or, to use the old term, confect) the sacraments and salvation. It also melds seamlessly with the Greek philosophical approach of John's Gospel where the *Logos* has the power to be generative too. When the

Logos becomes flesh, the potential of Divine creative power is shifted to a human body, which in turn leads to the ancient Christian theology of Theosis or Divinization. All of which means, in the Christian cultural world, words, and the actions they inspire and even manifest, can matter in an ultimate and eternal way.

WORDS AS THEY RELATE TO SILENCE

As we've said, a preacher is faced with two very distinct and very important jobs: First decide what message they want to say, and then decide how to deliver it. This book is not about the function of script writing, but important to note is that writing a book or a poem which will be read, usually in isolation, is not the same as writing for the spoken word, which an audience or congregation will hear rather than read. Writing a theological article for a magazine is not the same as writing to unpack that idea in a sermon.

On this subject, Pope Francis recently said:

> . . . And here I will say something that is linked to silence, but for priests. Please, the homilies: they are a disaster. At times I hear someone: "Yes, I went to Mass in that parish . . . yes, a good lesson of philosophy, forty, forty-five minutes . . . Eight, ten, no more!" And always a thought, a sentiment and an image. Let people take something home with them.[2]

You know there's a problem when even the pope admits it! But he also gives us four very useful guides for the writing portion of the work: Start with silence, and include a thought, a sentiment, and an image. In other words, something for the mind (a thought or idea), something for the heart (a sentiment or emotion), and something for the imagination (an image or a call to intuition). I believe the pope is saying: Address the whole person.

If we're going to address the whole person, then we need to speak with our own "whole person." The purpose? To communicate something the congregation can take home, something to help each person live through the coming days, just like one wants to leave a concert humming a tune. That something might be a renewed sense of joy, often in the face of a less-than-perfect reality. It might be a new perspective that helps you

---

2. https://www.vatican.va/content/francesco/en/speeches/2023/january/documents/20230120-vivere-pienezza-azione-liturgica.html.

unpack something going on in your world. Or it might be a challenge to be a different person going forward. The purpose of good ritual and good theater alike is to make a change for the better easier, no matter how small. To do that, the congregation or audience must internalize the message in some way.

We've dealt with some points about this above, but I want to address the starting point, silence, which I'm delighted Pope Francis recognized. It is the genesis point for both performers and clergy-types alike and underpins everything else.

The performer, the presider, and the preacher are there to deliver the script, and in so doing serve the author to the people. But the script is only words, notes, moves, and sometimes stage directions/rubrics. The meaning of the words and the significance of the stage directions are, as we'll see, in the silence and stillness *within* those words and actions. Four quotes from different fields help explain that this is a universal phenomenon.

> *The Music is not in the notes, but in the silence in between*
> —Wolfgang Mozart

> *A painter paints pictures on canvas, but a musician paints their pictures on silence.* —Leopold Stokowski

> *We're fascinated by the words, but where we meet is in the silence behind them.* —Ram Dass

> *In order to understand the dance one must be still, and in order to truly understand stillness one must dance.* —Rumi

Silence comes in two contrasting varieties: it can be the absence of noise or the presence of an energized quality. Similarly, stillness can be the absence of movement or the presence of a contained energy of possibility. Audiences and congregations can also experience the benefits of these two states. The good thing for all of us is that by doing the first version of both these qualities (by focusing on the absence of it), we can "fake it till we make it" for reaching the positive quality.

A practice which requires both, for example, is sitting yoga. I don't know anyone who's ever reached any sort of feeling or reality of "presence" or "quiet" very quickly. Usually long periods of just trying to be still and shut up, both regarding the external voice and, even harder, the internal one, tick by. Indeed, people who practice sitting yoga admit to needing to return to the basics on a daily basis. Yoga is an excellent example of "fake it till you make it" being a very acceptable spiritual and physical practice! In truth, it *is* the practice!

In the same way, a dancer spends hours a day over months and years doing "class" to have control of their body. Once they have some semblance of this, they can walk out onto a stage and stand very still, yet with a huge amount of possibility that might break out of their being at any moment, in any direction, yet always consciously placed and deliberate.

To add to this, I believe it's impossible to experience true stillness and silence without also taking notice of one's breath. Again, yoga makes this very clear, as do the better dance and acting teachers. And of course, voice coaches focus on this immensely.

One of the most ancient prayers in Christianity is the Jesus Prayer, very popular in both the Eastern and Western Churches, where one breathes in on the words "Lord Jesus Christ, Son of the Living God," and then breathes out on the traditional prayer "have mercy on me, a sinner." This mantra is repeated over and over in order to ground the individual in the loving presence of God and to acknowledge our created relationship with the Divine Other. Some people like to vary the prayer in personal ways, such as "have mercy on me, your child who is lost," or "be near to me who longs for your presence."

Most importantly with this prayer, one must learn to breathe deeply, from the diaphragm or the belly, not by taking a shallow breath into just the upper chest. This is also the breathing style which classical singers use, yoga teachers teach, and many other disciplines recommend too. One hopes seminary courses also teach it.

There's at least one parish I visited that begins their services with a guided breathing exercise/meditation before the opening greeting, with the ministers already in place. Members report finding the practice remarkably grounding and helpful to prayer, even though they were quite "chatty" before. Over the course of the celebration, one can move from silence to more active, overt participation, including laughter as appropriate, and back to silence when invited to do so. The lesson here is that silent stillness is not opposed to joyous community making; a place exists for both if organized and presented authentically. The lesson is, again, not a case of either/or but leaders learning how to manage the both/and. To do that, one has to be comfortable and experienced in the mediums of silence and stillness as much as we are with words and movement.

I have seen this many times in the theater, possibly the most memorable being in 1994 when the UK's National Theatre brought their production of *Medea* (not a happy play!) to New York. The title role was taken by the late Diana Rigg, famous to many of a certain age for her TV role in *The Avengers* in the 1960s, and for many others as Lady Olenna, Queen of Thorns in *Game of Thrones*. Expecting a Greek tragedy, I witnessed a New York audience (not normally an easy crowd) laughing with Medea/Diana as she used the text and the fluid actions of her face and body to turn the character's righteous anger and fear into a light, mocking manner which contrasted the male actors' rigidity and stiffness. This put the audience squarely on her side, which made the play's final scene, where—spoiler alert!—Medea massacres her children rather than lose them to her bully husband, all the more powerful.

By enabling an audience or congregation to laugh together, we're brought into the presence of the moment, because one cannot laugh or cry and *not* be present. When we laugh or cry, we've made a commitment to that particular moment. We've stepped out of our critical mind into a place of "being here, now." When we laugh or cry, we automatically breathe more deeply; indeed, we might actually be gasping for breath if we're doing either enthusiastically.

The purpose of training in stillness and silence for oneself, and the awareness of the importance of breath that goes with them, is therefore two-fold. Failing to develop these gifts for oneself contributes to being a less skillful practitioner when carrying any archetype, because one lacks conscious grounding, meaning the archetype tends to end up being presented as all about the externals (doing the appropriate thing), not essence (being the appropriate person). This is true whether one is a parent, teacher, doctor, etc., not just an actor or minister. Also, developing these gifts to any significant degree increases one's ability to lead a group (congregation, audience) by example into their own experience of them, and that's where they have a greater chance to experience the depth of the script around which they are gathering.

As the composer Claude Debussy (echoing Mozart) famously said, "Music is the space between the notes," so one can also say the meaning of words is the silence between and within them. This was demonstrated and explained excellently by the theater director Peter Brook in his book *The Empty Space*, based on four lectures he gave in the late 1960s covering various stages of theater (and also ritual) health, which he labeled Deadly, Holy, Rough, and Immediate. Brook's intention was to show a university audience how the role of actor and audience are connected. He asked for a volunteer and gave them a passage from the play *The Investigation* about Auschwitz. The passage described bodies in a gas chamber. Brook continues:

> As the volunteer took the paper and read it over to himself the audience tittered in the way an audience always does when it sees one of its kind on the way to making a fool of himself. But the volunteer was too struck and too appalled by what he was reading to react with the sheepish grins that are also customary. Something of his seriousness and concentration reached the audience and it fell silent. Then at my request he began to read out loud. The very first words were loaded with their own ghastly sense and the reader's response to them. Immediately the audience understood. It became one with him, with the speech—the lecture room and the volunteer who had come on to the platform vanished from sight—the naked evidence from Auschwitz was so powerful that it took over completely. Not only did the reader continue to speak in a shocked attentive silence, but his reading, technically speaking, was perfect—it had neither grace nor lack of grace, skill nor lack of skill—it was perfect because he had no attention to spare for self-consciousness, for wondering whether he was using the right intonation. He knew the audience wanted to hear, and he wanted to let them hear: the images found their own level and guided his voice unconsciously to the appropriate volume and pitch.

To contrast with this, Brook asked for a second volunteer and gave them the list of the English and French dead after the Battle of Agincourt from Shakespeare's *Henry V* to read. Brook continues:

> One look at the volume of Shakespeare had already set off a series of conditioned reflexes. . . . He put on a false voice that strived to be noble and historical, mouthed his words roundly, made awkward stresses, got tongue-tied, stiff, and confused, and the audience listened inattentive and restless. When he had done, I asked the audience why they could not take the list of dead at Agincourt as seriously as the description of death at Auschwitz. This provoked a lively exchange.
>
> > 'Agincourt's in the past.'
> > 'But Auschwitz is in the past.'
> > 'Only fifteen years.'
> > 'So how long's it got to take?'
> > 'When's a corpse a historical corpse?'
> > 'How many years make killing romantic?'

> *After this had gone on for some time, I proposed an experiment. The amateur actor was to read the speech again, stopping for a moment after each name: the audience was to endeavour silently in the pause to recall and put together its impressions of Auschwitz and Agincourt, to try to find a way of believing that these names were once individuals, as vividly as if the butchery had occurred in living memory. The amateur began to read again and the audience worked hard, playing its part. As he spoke the first name, the half silence became a dense one. Its tension caught the reader, there was an emotion in it, shared between him and them and it turned all his attention away from himself on to the subject matter he was speaking. Now the audience's concentration began to guide him: his inflexions were simple, his rhythms true: this in turn increased the audience's interest and so the two-way current began to flow. When this was ended, no explanations were needed, the audience had seen itself in action, it had seen how many layers silence can contain.*[3]

Our job as performer, presider or preacher is to "invite" the audience/congregation into a moment and then "give away" to them that which we are working on. Each person in attendance will take away something different depending on (a) where they are on their journey and (b) their ability to "take in" what's been offered, which in turn is a measure of their vulnerability to, and ability to integrate with, "the new."

We are responsible to develop and model an openness to this vulnerability within ourselves too, proving us to be trustworthy leaders into the unknown.

Pope Francis said something similar in the same address quoted above for those carrying the ministerial archetype:

> *... we must always keep the good of the communities, the pastoral care of the faithful (cf. Caeremoniale Episcoporum, 34) before our eyes, to lead the people to Christ and Christ to the people. It is the primary objective, which must be in first place also when you prepare and guide the celebrations. If we neglect this, we will have beautiful rites, but without strength, without flavour, without meaning, because they do not touch the heart and the existence of the people of God . . . It is Christ who stirs the heart; it is the encounter with him that attracts the Spirit. "A celebration that does not evangelize is not authentic" (Desiderio desideravi, 37). It is a "ballet," a beautiful ballet, aesthetic, beautiful, but (without this dimension of evangelization) it is not an authentic celebration.*

---

3. Brook, *Empty Space*, 24–25.

Or, to say something similar in theater terms: "All production, no content!" Lots of bells and whistles, and costumes (and egos probably), which aren't at the service of what the author, through the script, is trying to say and do.

Training oneself and others to be comfortable with silence and stillness is so important for our shared archetypes because that's where we connect our analytical self with the emotional self and, probably most importantly, our natural intuition, which includes the imagination. If we're so busy "doing" our job that we don't take time to "be" our self then we'll miss out on one of our most natural gifts and benefits, our unspoken unique talent that probably drew us to this work in the first place.

This teaches us that, simply put, I am me and not you, and you are you and not me, and yet we are here together. This statement, though again obvious, requires us to deal with two other realities. First, that I must keep my ego in check so that I don't think I can do everybody else's part as well as or better than they. Even if I could, the fact is irrelevant because, quite simply, I'm not doing their part, and that's the end of it. Second, that this is a communal effort of interlocking parts and the whole enterprise fails without the integration of the parts. An attachment to one's own brilliance may be the very cause of the whole enterprise failing. Someone's brilliance isn't the problem, but attachment to it can be, because it necessarily excludes and judges "the other" as less-than. A lack of generosity, at a personal or professional level, is a sign of not having done the work of exploring one's own journey into silence and stillness, the undergirding bedrock of communication and meaning, and therefore community and learning.

When one is starting to prepare for a new part in a play, beginning to write a new sermon, or working on creating a new ritual (and every one of them, even every ordinary Sunday, should have an element of "new" in it, presented "as if the ink were still wet"), we're invited to take time to start afresh. Take time to be silent and still, letting go of everything that's telling you, "Oh, I know the answer to this," or, "I know how to do this," or worst, "I can do what I did last time." The old adage that "one cannot step into the same river twice" reminds us that even if I believe "I" am the same as last time (which I'm most certainly *not*), no one else is. Even if I'm using a script I've used before, it's only that, a bunch of words on a page. The script is never the same as the play, the sermon, or the ritual. The script is just a script, the musical score is just a score. They are each a starting point of myriad journeys and destinations; and even if those destinations are all in a particular neighborhood, they are distinct. The practitioner needs to be aware and open to this before they start.

A simple exercise to experience how one script or manuscript can lead to different destinations is to pick a piece of music and listen to it performed by five or six different people or groups. Be it a Joni Mitchell song, a Stephen Sondheim piece, a Chopin nocturne, or a Tchaikovsky symphony, each performance will be, and indeed should be, unique.

We can explain this by reminding ourselves that, as we said at the beginning, every time we say "I love you" we mean something different. We mean "I love you" differently the first time we say it to a person than we do when we say it the hundredth time, or the last time at a final parting. Words are incredibly important, but they are only commonly agreed-upon symbols for communally-based items, people, things, or meanings. As Virginia Woolf said in her Essay "*Craftsman:* "Words do not live in a dictionary, they live in the mind." Scripts are a symbol picture book able to be read by folks who know that "language." However, language isn't the same as meaning. As we mentioned before, a "biscuit" is different in London than in New York, as is a jumper, a pavement, or a chip.

An audience and congregation can create powerful silence for themselves—hopefully you've experienced the expectancy before or within a play or a liturgy—but they aren't likely to maintain it if the same energy of expectant presence isn't returned from the stage or altar.

To repeat: Silence can be either the absence of noise or the presence of possibility. On the negative end, we've all probably been in situations where we or someone else was actively keeping a conversation going to avoid a deafening silence descending which could, frequently be embarrassing. Many people these days fill their lives with "something, anything" rather than live in silence. To see folks walking around in the 1970s and '80s carrying boomboxes on their shoulders wasn't uncommon; thereafter we had cassette recorders and then CD players with headsets. These days most people under forty (and many over) seem to have their earbuds inserted almost constantly, and phone calls are accessible almost anywhere on the planet. The most paradoxical occasion is when someone's gone for a walk or run in nature to "clear their head," only to insert their earbuds for the entire trip. I'm constantly reminded of the rhetorical question a wise teacher once observed: "I know we can, and that's wonderful, but should we?"

The inability to engage silence is, I fear, right up there with the pope's need to suggest homilies be reduced to eight to ten minutes; people have supposedly lost the ability to pay attention, though they want to be continually engaged, distracted, or entertained. When people ask how I can manage to live most days without the radio playing, I usually like to respond, "Well, I have so many conversations going on in my head, it'd be rude to interrupt them." However, given the challenge that it's difficult to invite folks to change, we must learn to meet them where they are. We must also ensure that what we have to say is sufficiently engaging (informative, entertaining, gripping, awe-inspiring, or scarily truthful) that folks can't help but pay attention. To say that silence is the dimension that both words and breath share is not hyperbole; it is the basis for anything and everything we want to communicate.

While most public speakers have a sense of how what they're saying is "coming across," and will adapt their pitch, breathing, and pauses (and especially longer dramatic silences) to alter their delivery as they "read the room," when it comes to working with a script, different practices apply. When we're working with a set script, and especially scripture or prayers, we tend to assume the punctuation provided by the author, translator, or editor is our guide. This isn't necessarily the case. Most modern liturgical scripts seem to be written to be read rather than spoken, which is very wrong-headed, as they'll mainly be used as spoken texts. However, there are exceptions. One of the reasons so many people still love the old King James Version of the Bible is that it flows off the tongue so naturally—at least, it does if you're used to seventeenth-century English. The original writing committee achieved this by agreeing that the final test to be given to every single verse of translation, covering the whole collection of books the Bible contained, was that they should be read aloud to the group, and "land on the ear" in the way they intended.

While a very practical reason existed for this prioritizing of the spoken word (including that most people in England still couldn't read for themselves, so the translation committee wanted the people to hear something they could understand and remember), an equally strong theological reason existed, which we mentioned above. While the Bible is held by Christians to be the inspired Word of God, it is not, especially in translation and often after transliterations, considered to be the actual *words* of God. Theologically the presence of God in Scripture is based on the idea of the people hearing the Divinely inspired words land on their ears, carried by the invisible breath and air. As the recipients of the word coming into their ears, they become the ones who are potentially touched by God's grace. Again, as mentioned above, this echoes the opening of the Bible's first book, Genesis, where God's spoken words ("Let there be . . .") is generative because they were carried on Ruah—the breath of God, a symbol of the Holy Spirit (a word, incidentally, which is feminine in Hebrew).

While some traditions and communities have understandably venerated actual copies of the book which we call The Holy Bible, the theological tradition is actually much more concerned with the living word which it contains, which only becomes "living" when it's spoken out loud and heard. When copies of the book are honored because they're a physical representation, a symbol of the contents, honoring that symbol is not the same as honoring those contents when they're proclaimed. After all, for almost 100 percent of the time, what is proclaimed is in translation or transliteration, so not in any way the original words, just an attempt at a more-or-less culturally appropriate meaning. The Word that matters is ultimately not the ones of the page but the One which lands on our ear and travels to our hearts and minds, and is not based on any human language, even ancient Hebrew, Greek, or Aramaic. These written words matter, and are the vehicle for the meaning, but they're not the same.

When, as ministers, we understand this ancient theological point both intellectually as well as experientially, then we have a new insight into why a script is not the same as a play, a liturgical text is different from a prayer, and the typed words of a homily is not the same as the received experience of hearing one preached.

To put it another way, receiving a card which says "I love you" is very nice, but much more powerful is when someone stands (or kneels) in front of you, looks you in the eye and says it directly. No? The simple fact is that none of these texts—a play, a prayer, a set of sermon notes—contain breath or silence. That only comes when they are enfleshed or incarnated.

Furthermore, one important point about the difference between silence as presented in writing (we are, after all, talking about jobs which require us to use scripts) and silence as it happens in actual speech is that when we speak we don't necessarily follow the punctuation of the written word. While an experienced playwright might build this into the script in one of several ways, those who write scripts for worship generally don't. When liturgical texts are analyzed, they're reviewed as written texts, not spoken ones. The one who's going to "incarnate" them must understand this reality. Most written liturgical texts are presented as if more than one interpretation of what is being said weren't meant, so the liturgist or preacher need not leave space for personal styling. This is incorrect.

While the words might have gone through various committees and approvals, there isn't, nor has there ever been, a standardized way to present the intention, and the silence in the words.

The same is true in normal conversations, where we might use pauses when we speak to give emphasis, or we might take a breath when no comma (in the written version) exists to give us space to think of the right word. This difference between written and spoken words cannot be over-emphasized.

I again remember Rev. Dr. Margie Brown telling us to "never forget that a sermon or homily is not a monologue but a dialogue between you and the congregation, and the silences are where the congregation has time to think and internally respond." It's the same with theatrical soliloquies, which might be spoken by one person, but addressed to the audience and therefore effectively become a dialogue. I should note that we were largely a Caucasian class, so I'm sure Dr. Brown wouldn't have assumed an unspoken response if she were working with preachers from mainly black churches, whose voiced responses of "Amen" and other affirmations come from a depth of feeling and culture which cannot remain silent. I've had the joy of attending churches where the congregation was predominantly African American, and their depth of feeling is a wonderful and powerful experience to witness.

If an actor or minister wants to learn how to play with silence for its own sake as well as within words, a great place to start is with contemporary poetry, a helpful vehicle for learning how to create space around and within words. The works of Mary Oliver and David Whyte are widely available online and provide pieces to which most if not all people can relate, therefore making it easy for a person to find their version of the feelings behind the words. David's work is also available as audio files, reading several pieces of his own and other poets. One note, however: It takes courage to put those feelings into one's voice.

Scripture too has poetry in it, and one of the most heard is Paul's words in 1 Cor. 13:4–8, often used at weddings. Unfortunately, it's too often "massacred" in the delivery, as if Paul were writing a dogmatic list of requirements against which we will be judged and found wanting rather than an inspiration for joy. In church when people see something is by Paul, they seem to go to "stern school principal" voice rather than a "wise old kind grandparent" one. The former "voice" is telling us what to do and not do, while the latter is trying to inspire us with what to desire, and let our actions follow our intuitions and feelings. If you're interested in a simple experiment, try reading this short piece in both voices (stern school principal and then kindly grandparent) and try to notice where in your body your breath (and therefore voice) is coming from.

> *Love is patient, love is kind.*
> *It does not envy, it does not boast,*
> *it is not proud.*
> *It does not dishonor others,*
> *it is not self-seeking,*
> *it is not easily angered,*
> *it keeps no record of wrongs.*
> *Love does not delight in evil but rejoices with the truth.*
> *It always protects,*
> *always trusts,*
> *always hopes,*
> *always perseveres.*
> *Love never fails.*

My experience of doing the experiment is that my "stern school principal" voice is at the back of my throat and is more projected, as if I'm speaking to a class of miscreant 14-year-olds. This voice is curt and direct, as if I'm working hard to get the message across. My "kindly grandparent voice," on the other hand, is lower, warmer, and breathier. I also feel like my eyes are smiling knowingly, as if I'm sharing secrets learned from long years of relationships, with both their successes and failures, and this lifts my cheekbones, so I'm also actually smiling a little too. This voice also reads more slowly and finds breaks in the text beyond the punctuation.

While you'll experience different silences within each reading, you'll also probably be aware of the silence within you that is different for each "voice."

Most scripture in churches is read by laity who are frequently not required to have any training, so these exercises shouldn't be limited to just the official church leaders. I have led many lector or reader workshops for parishes where each person was invited to proclaim before their peers one of the passages they'd been assigned for the coming season. It was very important that each person not just receive comments, but also give them to each other. Before we finished I had them "buddy up" so that they had a built-in cheerleader and kindly observer to help them receive feedback and learn over time. Someone almost always reads a piece from Paul, and I frequently use the exercise mentioned. The reaction from their peers is always everything needed. The second time the lector gives themself permission to speak from a different place, and almost always receives great affirmation from the group that this way of speaking gets the message over in a way they, as the congregation, are willing to listen to. The communication is more effective because the speaker is sharing from a place of relationship that is rich in the willingness to suffer, and to prevent suffering, for the other. A loving suffering often born out of parenting, service and lost loves. To use Peter Brook's phrase, the group "had seen how many layers silence may contain."

WORDS AS THEY RELATE TO STILLNESS

In the same way that silence can be an absence or presence, so stillness can be the absence of movement or the real presence of a tangible quality.

Stillness can be a very powerful and useful "movement capability" to add to one's toolkit. There are teachers who have perfected the art of walking into a classroom and just standing there until the students are quiet, and it's amazing to see and can be quite an intimidating experience!

Like a dancer or someone doing yoga (although I suppose actually "not doing" would be more accurate), the stillness we are seeking is full of potential. Scripture talks fondly of the "still, small, voice of calm" which followed the wind, the earthquake and the fire, and that only there could Elijah hear God's voice (1Kings 19:11–13). So often people (both onstage and in the sanctuary) think they have to "do more" when, in fact, "more" has to be in a dynamic relationship with "less," and even nothing (best thought of here as "no-thing"). Without that silence and stillness, the author's voice (and God's Spirit) can't move through the space between the words.

In all these examples, learning to carry a real presence requires us to grow in stillness. To extroverts this seems to favor those on the more introverted energy end of the personality spectrum, where stillness may seem more natural, even though several introverted friends say it is not. Either way, the challenge is to create a presence for potential.

For those on the more extroverted energy end of the scale, along with folks who have, for example ADHD, it can feel like an unfair challenge. These folk more easily manifest "potential action," but less easily a calm moment. For them the invitation is to find out what they need to do to gain a similar quality in their communication toolkit by asking, "What does the positive quality of 'stillness' look like in my body?" One possible answer is finding how "stillness" can be created as the gap between movements, and then learning how to intensify that moment by becoming more conscious of it, and, for some, not fearing it. These alternative examples of finding "stillness" are equivalent to physical mantras, which can work very similarly to vocal and verbal ones for creating a space full of possibility into which words can be spoken. Think of the rhythmic drumming of a Native American pow-wow or a walking meditation as examples. Into such a "moving stillness" a body can step more freely and openly.

I have been very fortunate to have worked with colleagues across the introvert/extrovert scale and have learned from all of them. However, they do approach acting as well as religion and spirituality differently. We forget this at our peril as our audiences and congregations, at least potentially, are quite definitely spread over a very wide range of the scale, if not the entirety of it.

In the entertainment field, popular concerts and productions are more and more about special effects, multi-dimensional engagement, and stimulation, with louder volumes and bigger and bigger crowds. This is a heavenly playland for those on the more extroverted end of the energy scale, but would be hell on earth for an introvert. When one adds to this the fact that many have a tendency to become more introverted and traditional as we age, it points to a natural attraction between these forms of engagement and the younger, outward leaning part of the population. Some non-liturgical churches have been following this model, with specialty lighting, more engaged music, and the "sing-along" approach of those concerts. Many have seen significant growth in this same demographic of younger, more extroverted folks. A catchphrase for this group might be those looking for "participatory engagement."

The traditional liturgical churches, along with more classical music concerts and more serious plays (dramas as opposed to comedy and musicals), tend to be a more welcoming place for folks at the more introverted end of the energy scale. A catchphrase for this group might be folks who prefer "reflective engagement." Many, of course, enjoy both experiences.

While opportunities abound between these two extremes, unfortunately both groups, in the sad habit of our humanity, tend to ridicule the other group for being "not my group." The epithets are easy to hear: "You're old-fashioned." "You have no taste." "It's so loud." "You're living in the past." "Your generation has lost the ability to reflect." And don't even start to try to compare an organ in church with an electric guitar and drum set! This is yet another manifestation of either/or thinking as opposed to both/and.

OUR PERSONAL RELATIONSHIP WITH SILENCE AND STILLNESS

When we add to this dichotomy the sad reality that both the theater and the churches (as opposed to personal spirituality) are intimately linked to making money to pay the bills, (unfortunate but true!) we can see the writing on the wall against structural integration unless we chose to stand firm for something that includes both sides, regardless of the consequences, especially the financial ones. This means, interestingly, that we're actually not that far removed from the reality of most of history, where sponsorship, having wealthy patrons, and the sad tradition of selling perceived benefits (whether casting someone's kid in a play for a sizeable "donation" or selling indulgences) are necessary to balance the books on the temporal side of the balance sheet.

If this is the "Bad News," what is the "Good?"

I was once giving a series of evening talks in a parish on liturgical change in mainstream Christianity, and was sharing some options for what might be possible for this community as they deal with dwindling numbers and too much space and debt. The first reaction from one of the frequently outspoken members was, unsurprisingly, "Well, I don't like that idea." This was a person with whom I had a very good relationship and so was able to smile and say, "I never expected for a moment that you would, but I'm afraid 'I don't like it' isn't a valid liturgical or spiritual judgment criteria in this situation." I'm pleased to say we both laughed!

Having said that, "I don't like it" is a very valid decision criteria when a person or group is deciding where they want to go for entertainment, spiritual growth, or a community of peers. We may need to have our expectations challenged every now and again but, rather like those green beans from childhood, the adult in me knows that if I've tried it and it doesn't work for me, then I'm free to say, "No thank you." Alternatively, if it does work for me, then I can make a commitment to go back. Also, I can always change my mind!

The "Good News" therefore is that in the "no spin" place that is silence and grounded stillness, we learn to be honest about what is objective truth and what is subjective truth. In this way, a loud concert by a popular band, with lasers, light show, and 50,000 people present, all singing and chanting "Save the World," might be an objective good, yet that I still don't want to go but others do is okay.

This sort of silence and internal stillness is, one quickly realizes, great for peace and consensus building, and bad for maintaining conflict, which is the essence of drama. This is why a good actor works to try to understand what lies a character is telling themself to maintain their status quo. In the play, catharsis can come when the actor/character in some way opens the internal barrier to the larger truth they had feared to access. In this way the actor is, of course, mirroring for the audience what we all do if we're not aware of our own internal barriers and prejudices. Too often this internal surrender to the truth comes, theology would suggest, with death, real or imagined, a small one or the final one, both on stage and in life. The more we work on these issues when we're alive, the less conflicted each of those "small ends," as well as that big "final end," might be.

When an actor has to play a conflicted person as their character, that is a bonus which makes the job engaging. When a minister is required to hide that same reality, it's a great sadness. In the theater we assume a humanity that is heterogeneous, full of differences. In the churches we seem to be wanting to create a world that is remarkably homogeneous, which isn't what we see in the model of creation around us. It is only when we see the churches and the different faiths and indigenous traditions brought together that we see more of humanity potentially reflected and we learn just how "big" the Divine Other might be. If a person has a very small version of God in their heart, then growing in a faith and understanding which is *always* inclusive will be a challenge.

This reality, of like gathering with like and avoiding opposites, has been noticed by philosophers for a while, with Fredrick Nietzsche probably being the most relevant for our discussion when he covered it in his book *The Birth of Tragedy*. Interestingly, Nietzsche began his professional career in the field of philology, which is the study of language from ancient texts and scripts, including the earliest Greek and Roman plays of which we have copies.

Briefly, *The Birth of Tragedy* explores the way ancient Grecco-Roman society saw the Greek god brothers Apollo and Dionysius (both sons of Zeus from different mothers) as balancing each other and indeed needing each other, whereas modern society (he was writing in the late 1800s) sees them as offering an "either-or" for the way forward. Apollo had become the "good guy" because he represents logic and the classical arts, honor, harmony, progress, and the principle of individuation, and had been a good fit for individual salvation in the Christian model. Dionysius, on the other hand, represented disorder, intoxication, emotion, ecstasy, and unity (aka crowd mentality), a good fit for what we would today call "populism" and a decidedly "bad fit" for anyone remotely involved with Christianity. Added to this, Dionysius (known as Bacchus to the Romans) was the god to whom incense was offered at the beginning of any theatrical performance in the Roman Empire of early Christianity, and hence the diatribes from many early Christian writers and theologians, famously including Tertullian (c.155–220 CE) who basically equated actors with everything that was morally wrong with the world. If the theater was for Dionysius, the lustful drunkard, then the church would be for Apollo, the sun god! And so, the separation in Christianity between mind and body, thought and feelings began, and the development of the iconography of a sun god being like the Son of God developed.

The attitude that "sex and also any fun involving food or drink are bad" can be found in many of the letters attributed to St. Paul, as well as in the early "Church Fathers" such as Tertullian, and of course Augustine 200 years later. While Apollo represented the logical way "good" people have always done things, Dionysius can be seen as representing the experimenters, the unorthodox, the risk takers, the embodied people who liked to play. Apollo was the head (like Jesus) and Dionysius was the body (seen by some as the sinful flesh from the neck down).

Bearing this in mind, we can maybe see why mainline Christianity has never really had the chance to develop a reasonable integrated sense of mind *and* body, and why it remains a living paradox to profess an incarnated Son of God yet not knowing what to do with the rest of our human bodies before they're dead except to try to control them. I suspect that what we can do is hope to recognize the depth of the paradox in which we're living. It'd be wonderful if our connection with the creative arts could be the vehicle for a new understanding of how the ancient mythical brothers continue to live in their obvious creative tension in each of us today. If we can learn it for ourselves, we then have a chance to share it with the world.

QUESTIONS FOR REFLECTION

1. Are you aware of your personality type through any of the standard aids, such as the Meyers-Briggs Personality Indicator or the Enneagram, etc.? Are you aware of how your personality interacts with the requirements of your work? When it helps and when it hinders?
2. When are you most yourself? When do you feel most aware of the Divine in dialogue with you?
3. What is your relationship with your physical and sexual body?
4. When you preach or preside, to what extent are you aware of being yourself or of hiding yourself?

7

The Role of the Audience/ Community as Critics and Sustainers

Written on a page, words are a text or script. Spoken out loud, they are a cry to be heard, which needs an audience.

IF YOU HANG AROUND theater folks much, you're sure to hear the phrase: "There are no small parts, only small actors." To which you might also hear the response: "There are no small actors, only small wage packets."

If you've ever been to a one-person show, whether theater, music, or comedy night, and you look at the program, you'll undoubtedly see a list of other people without whom the show would not have gone on, whether that's only three or four names or closer to a dozen or two. And of course no show can exist without an audience, because that's called a "rehearsal." Indeed, an old theater tradition dictates that the show does in fact not need to go on if more people are onstage than are in the audience.

A CONGREGATION MIRRORS AN AUDIENCE

For the performing arts, the need for an audience is in the title; we need an audience to make it a performance. Talk to any performer and they'll tell you that the effect on the performance of an audience is significant. First, as soon as an audience appears, the performer feels different because, among other things, internal chemicals are triggered. Adrenalin and other hormones start pumping, and electrical connections are made. This may be beneficial or deleterious, or both in an alternating swell, but real effects will ensue. One hears some famous and well-established actors talk publicly about being almost sick before walking on stage, even after forty years of doing the job, which does make me wonder if presiders ever feel that way. And if not, why?

Regardless of the discipline, every performance is fundamentally about communication involving three components: the originator, the medium, and the receiver. The originator might be a composer, choreographer, or writer, dead or alive, who might also be part or all of the medium, for example a stand-up comedian who writes all their own material. The medium, whom we could also call the interpreter, is the connector between the original creative impulse and the end receiver of the message. The medium's job (as actor, musician, dancer, speaker, etc.) is to do everything in their power to ensure that what they believe the originator was trying to express is delivered as effectively and totally as possible. One thing to notice here is that, unless you are both the originator and the medium, doing this job is impossible without the act of interpretation. And unless you're a self-directed solo performer, any performance needs a director or conductor-type person to ensure the interpretation is consistent across all the performers.

The good news/bad news about interpretation is that it can be enlightening or confusing, "on the mark" or way off. It can open up hidden depths in a piece or it can obfuscate even the most obvious intention. Interpretation can be at the service of the originator or the self-service of the one doing the interpretation. Interpretation is always a risk and always an opportunity. One universal truth seems clear, however: to agree to be in the role of the medium or interpreter and not take the responsibilities seriously is courting disaster. One might do it badly, lacking skill or experience and with poor results; but if one is at least aware that choices need to be made because nothing is obvious, one is at least acting with good intent, or so we hope.

Why is this fact so important? Because, like the old adage that one cannot step into the same river twice, words and notes and even movements that were transferred to paper once upon a time can't be brought back in their original condition when one has changed the time, place, and medium. This is even true when one is working with originators who are their own mediums, like a pianist playing their own work. Even for them (ask Elton John, for example, or Lady Gaga), creating the same exact experience twice is impossible.

There are classical musicians who like to play music only on the instruments of the same period as the piece, and hearing them is fascinating, though usually a much different experience from listening to the same piece played on contemporary equivalents. This is a choice that can add to our experience. But to forbid any other options wouldn't be good. For example, Bach's famous Toccata and Fugue in D minor is amazing on the organ of an ancient church or cathedral, with its resonant acoustics and, if one is lucky, a thirty-two-foot-long bass pipe. But the work is also amazing when heard on a solo guitar or an Indonesian gamelan. In this way, every performance isn't just an interpretation but also an act of culturalization. This is like the function of the preacher or prophet, pointing the way forward based on, but not limited by, the past and recognizing the uniqueness of a present context.

Because (a) the work being presented strives to have a coherent unity, and (b) a reliable team must bring the interpretation to fulfillment every time, practitioners of the performing arts know they're no less a part of a team than are soccer or baseball players. Even with this awareness, as we've said, without an audience their work is just another rehearsal, because the purpose for which the work was created hasn't been delivered to the intended place, the audience members' senses.

Regarding the audience of such performances, another theater adage is that "the audience gets the performance it deserves." This is because the degree to which an audience responds to the prompts of the performance, co-creating the act of communication, makes a significant difference to the results. One can reference again the earlier quote from Peter Brook about the audience seeing itself in action and how, when it did its work, it brought something more out of the performer.

To be fair, it's by no means always that easy. Sometimes one has to persuade and even seduce an audience into reaction and then action; it doesn't necessarily happen automatically. On the positive side, the audience has usually come voluntarily and has paid to be there, so they actively want to get something for their money and have hopes for an engaging performance. On the flip side they may also have (consciously or not) expectations and preferences. Theatre regulars will have heard someone say "that's not how I remembered it" on exiting a show, or that the casting didn't repeat previous productions. (The furor from a certain section of the population over a black actor being cast as Hermione in the London production of *Harry Potter and the Cursed Child* or Ariel in *The Little Mermaid* film remake are recent examples.)

Choosing to take a new look and go in a new direction with a script is an example of that necessary "interpretation" and "inculturation" function which a director brings to a production. Sometimes the interpretation is about changing the historical context; for example, moving a production of Wagner's early opera *Rienzi* from the context of the 1300s to Mussolini's Rome of the 1930s. I've seen such a "time translation" and it made the piece much easier to relate to, because I knew the story of Mussolini already, which gave the production a "way in" to my consciousness. I'm not a Wagner fan as such, so you'll have to ask others if (and what) was lost in the translation, but for me it helped rather than hindered my engagement and enjoyment, and I applauded the results.

Sometimes it's about a deeper change, for example changing the gender or sexuality of a character or group of characters. One could certainly claim this was changing the originator's intention, especially if a piece is out of copyright, in which case no legal recourse is available and no way to get authorization or even an opinion from them. As I said earlier, interpretation is a risk, and sometimes the risks aren't successful. However, that might also depend on how one defines "success." If success is selling seats and making money, that's quantifiable. If success is shifting a social norm and set of expectations, then it can be defined differently by different groups. I've seen productions that have done this, and in my very subjective eyes, some have succeeded wonderfully while others seemed pointless and even detrimental to the script. Yet at other times I wasn't bothered nor did the changes make much difference to my attention or reaction to the production if the performances were convincing.

Audiences can be very fickle or sensitive to changes in pieces which they hold dear. We therefore need to bring a discussion about "expectations" into the conversation about communication. Most of us don't like being taken by surprise in a situation. So, if a piece of poetry or music means a lot to us and we have an emotional connection to it, but someone "messes around with it" in a way which we don't like, we're likely to be upset and even angry with the interference.

We see how this can apply to the lives of both church and theater communities in their reactions when directors and pastors try to introduce change or something new. This has always been the case; many theater and music pieces now considered classics (such as Beethoven's later works, operas such as Bizet's *Carmen* and Rossini's *The Barber of Seville*, or Stravinsky's *The Rite of Spring*) were booed and in the latter case caused riots when they premiered. People who decried the music of The Beatles sixty years ago now dance happily to it and sing along at their grandchildren's weddings today.

As we've said, audiences and congregations are frequently self-selective. We tend to go where we believe our values and opinions won't be challenged. We largely socialize with these same groups. We do, as we heard both Gustav Mahler and Richard Rohr OFM say, like to be "comfortable" and even "cozy." But when, as leaders, we condition our communities (theatrical or religious) to only ever getting what they think they want, we fall very quickly back into creating Herschel's "heirlooms" and not "living fountains."

However, the other side of the reality is also true. While an audience or congregation is essential for the act of theater or liturgy, how they engage and participate can significantly change the way a particular gathering might be experienced. They can also derail it if it offends their sense of "what was meant to happen." This means that a pastor or director can't ignore what they believe to be, in church terms, the *sensus fidelium* (sense of the faithful) or its worldly equivalent, which we might call "popular taste." Just as the *sensus fidelium* of a group of Christians might not be theologically or historically grounded, so the popular taste of an audience might not be very well informed or enlightened. We are very much back to the realm of "I know what I like" and "we've never done it that way before."

Here again is that quote mentioned before from the document "Environment and Art in Catholic Worship" about the intent of liturgy: "God does not need liturgy, people do." However, what people need and what they like can frequently be two different things. The consequence of this reality is that almost every pastor and director must work in a dynamic tension (which is a constructive way to say "under stress") when bringing anything new to their respective congregation or audience. The first time one reads a script or outline for an act of worship, the needs, expectations, and likely reaction of the "people" is almost always a character in the room. The only ones totally free from this stress are those who are financially independent and have no need for the affirmation of others, willing to never work again in the same field if it all goes wrong. In other words, only the ones willing to be prophets in their field (false as much as true) are usually free enough to present their understanding of the truth for all to see. Most pastors and directors prefer to "play it safe" and protect the bottom line and/or their job.

Yet in the current era of falling attendance and the need for a new evangelization a powerful warning is to be heard. Every pastor needs to remember this truth: Everything you're doing to keep your congregation in the pews is exactly what's keeping everybody else out.

A well-known dictum states the work of Christian ministry is to "comfort the afflicted and afflict the comfortable." Yet a minister's job is also to help the people pray and learn on their life journey. To both challenge and comfort at the same time is very hard. Sometimes ministers are called to walk the "middle way" and be the bridge between differing views for the way forward, balancing new vision and old tradition. Some of us have this gift in abundance, others of us less so. I've known too many situations where leaders have been faced with the choice of doing what they feel is the right thing and losing a significant set of members and therefore donors, or backing down and keeping financial stability intact. Pray never to be in this position!

For this reason, the "new" rarely comes from the established communities of church or theater, from the "inner circles" of their respective sacred traditions or "what we've always done." Inviting folks to move out of the comfortable and cozy is risky. However, the good news is that both structures have created their own "experimental communities" on which the wise minds of the inner circles keep an eye. Theater festivals, especially ones that promote new works or fringe productions, are popular sources for the "next movement," as are places like university campus ministries and youth camp summer schools for the church folk.

We're back to the wisdom mentioned earlier from symphony orchestra management: "Give them a lot of what they want and a little of what's good for them." That's much easier when you're choosing three to five items for an evening's entertainment, and you can slip in one new piece. From the pastor's perspective slipping in something new is not that easy. A single new song is probably not going to cause a walkout, but similarly that new song is not going to be enough to bring in the outsider. Many pastors I know express the feeling of being caught between "maintenance and mission," between providing what the remaining people in the pews want (and, let's be honest, are paying for) against exploring what might be of interest to the nones, the un-churched and the ex-churched, who need something completely different, though can rarely express what that might be. (While churchgoers "know what they like," the unchurched tend to think in terms of "knowing what they don't like.")

Theater companies might try to add one lesser-known piece into a year's season, but most don't have the financial stability to produce four to six weeks of poor attendance without significant commercial or private sponsorship. The risk is too great. (Interesting fact: Even in good times, ticket sales only account for about 40% of the costs for most performance companies. All the rest is sponsorships and donations.) Yet without someone taking these risks, nothing ever changes. In which situation, science clearly confirms (as in the Law of Inertia mentioned before,) that something that never changes is either dying or is already dead. And when something which is much loved (an "heirloom") begins to die, much grief and anger follows.

This is one reason the Christian world was shocked and variously enlivened or enraged with Vatican II back in the 1960s. A huge change was commanded "from above" for the Roman Church, or so it seemed. In fact, conversations and recommendations for small changes in many fields had been going on for decades among those in the inner circles, including in Rome with the reading of, among other things, Rosmini's "Five Wounds" mentioned earlier. Yet there is hope too. An "inner circle" had created a very traditional agenda for that council, but at the first full meeting of the world's Catholic bishops they threw it out and wrote their own much more progressive one. Rebellion and renewal can come in the most unlikely places!

As I'm writing this book, the United Methodist Church is going through a major split on the issue of sexuality, the Southern Baptist Convention is doing the same over the role of women in ministry, and Pope Francis' "Synod on Synodality—Part Two" is underway in Rome, garnering mixed reviews. All this might be a prophetic moment for change and transformation in the years ahead. In all these cases the *sensus fidelium* has been strategically sought out, and the re-evaluation of attitudes to collegiality along with gender, celibacy, and sexuality explored. The results in all these cases seem to be pointing to a new world where denominations will either choose to learn to "agree to disagree" within themselves as much as with each other, or they go through a split or internal schism. As the world becomes smaller and science points to the unity of all creation, we humans seem to have to find smaller and yet smaller communities with which to identify. Identity is becoming more and more important to the people who seem to fear getting lost in the mix. And fear is a powerful motivation.

While this current "conflab" is largely about gender and sexuality, that's not really the issue at the root, just as services and the Bible in Latin wasn't 500 years ago during the Reformation, or the "*filioque*" 500 years before that, when the Eastern and Western churches went through their schism. At root humans have a problem not owning and controlling the Divine. The spiritual gift of surrender and humility is, I've observed, the last one most of us learn and accept when faced with a God who is so much bigger than we can comprehend. Ancient religions tried to appease the gods, and in this way control them. Jesus said we are adopted daughters and sons, and as such we love fighting over the rights to the inheritance, even though the disciples had that discussion with Jesus, and it didn't end well. (Mt. 18:1–5, Lk. 9:46–48, Mk. 10:35–45). Every one of us is an Eve and Adam, tempted to eat from a tree, The Knowledge of Good and Evil, whose fruit we ultimately cannot digest.

This changing reality can't be ignored by individual churches or theater companies, because these are issues about which their local people are concerned, one might even say afraid. The problem is that the root of the gospel message as well as the natural movement of artistic creation is towards the fullness of truth and the future, not the past and safety. Leaders are being asked (putting it rather dramatically, I admit), "What price for your soul?" The conflict between maintenance and mission isn't going to get any easier. If ever Christian churches (and everyone else) needed to spend time reflecting on Jesus' frequent post-resurrection command "do not be afraid," and to work out what it is we really fear, that time might be now.

The present reality, of course, doesn't come out of nowhere. Looking back over the past hundred years, we can see a series of moments of evolution and then very occasional moments of revolution. Evolution and revolution are almost the same words on the page (just one letter added!) but remarkably different when one lives through one or the other. In the theater we can see similar significant changes even over the same time span, from Edwardian Vaudeville, with rather static, stylized productions of the classics, to theater in the round, multi-racial casting, and gender-swapping roles. All these changes resulted in casualties of careers and livelihoods as well as new opportunities and developments.

However, throughout these sweeps of history, the hugely important role of prophetic leaders and their audiences or congregations has been utterly significant and determining. Without sufficient support from the latter, none of the changes would've been sustainable. We have, therefore, a conundrum, with the audience/congregation playing both very positive, supportive roles at times, as well as very conserving, restraining roles at others. This tension is also present at every performance and every service. At some level, every person in the church pew or theater seat is saying, "I want to be engaged." That engagement may be about being entertained or enlightened, it may be about being soothed or stimulated, or some combination of these and more. However, one can't deny that the audience/congregation is there with a need. Our job is to judge if we wish to answer that need, and help them scratch that itch, or tell them to get their needs met somewhere else. The Book of Exodus has several moments when Moses was faced with a similar issue, and in some ways things haven't changed that much.

WORKING TOGETHER AND THE GIFT OF HINDSIGHT

From about the fifth century to the 1950s, the main purpose of church was, as we've said, to help us avoid spending eternity in hell. The message was, "Though life is hard and full of suffering, wait until you try an unprepared death!"

Dionysian theater, hugely popular in the pre-Christian world, made a sanitized comeback in the ninth and tenth centuries with a brief Easter morning chanted *tableaux vivant* known as the "*Quem quaeritis?*" (Latin for the angels' words of "Whom do you seek.") This found its way into the liturgy to mark the journey of the three Marys to the tomb (Jn. 20:1, Mt. 28:1, Lk. 24:10). Interestingly, the other creative arts had thrived in the meantime. Paintings adorned many church walls, early stained-glass windows were beginning to appear, vestments had become more ornate and threaded with gold and silver (for the churches of the wealthy), and of course music and illustrated calligraphy in manuscripts were held in very high regard. Eventually the performing arts were forgiven and the ancient divide between "theater" and "church" has now been bridged for nearly a thousand years, each fueling the other in different ways.

Relatively quickly after the "*Quem quaeritis?*", as we mentioned earlier, we see throughout Europe the development of other religiously themed dramas, frequently moving out of the church building to the streets and marketplace. These popularly include what we call the Mystery (sometimes called Passion) and Miracle plays, depicting stories of the Bible (both Jewish and Christian parts, aka the "Old" and "New" Testaments) together with Morality (or Everyman) plays. By 1210 these had become so popular and elaborate, full of characters and costumes, that the pope at the time (Innocent III) issued an edict to stop the clergy acting in them. This led to the plays being taken over by lay groups, usually the local professional guilds, and sometimes troupes of traveling actors. The oldest extant script in English for a morality play (of which there is just one known copy) is a personal favorite, *The Castle of Perseverance*, from about 1420. We even have the set designs and costume suggestions for this very significant production, usually performed during Lent or for a major feast like Corpus Christi, (which celebrates Jesus' gift of himself to us in communion), complete with processions through the streets. This was a production of about three and a half hours, all in rhyming stanzas of Middle English involving five stages set in a circle around the eponymous castle, around which the standing audience was thought to move, following the action from stage to stage. The directions for the setting of the final stage—the Court of Heaven—dictates that it should be in the east of the circle and have an unobstructed view of the light from the setting sun so that God's and the angels' robes glistened in its rays. They tried to think of everything!

These grand productions were, unsurprisingly, incredibly popular, and became very important spiritually to the local communities, largely because they were engaging and in their language, while church services were in Latin with minimal or no participation. We should also add that they were economically beneficial to the merchants and tavern owners who catered to the folks who came to town for what was probably the only "professional" entertainment available all year.[1]

While the church might teach one set of understandings and definitions about what worship is, the human need to be engaged, to see ourselves reflected in the story, and to have the chance to "play" with characters is also very real. This is, again, not about either-or but both-and. While a solely monastic-style liturgy might work for the majority of clergy and a minority of the population, the majority of the population needs to balance that with action, engagement, and creativity. Jesus was, after all, part of a long tradition of rabbinical and cultural storytellers who continue to use all the skills available to them to get their message across.

So what is the work of the ministers of liturgy in regard to the congregation? God, as we have said, needs nothing—not our praise, not our attention, not our adoration. Christianity has always asked us to do these

---

1. If you wish to explore these ancient plays and themes, Radius, the Religious Drama Society of Great Britain has many resources, mainly online. RadiusDrama.org.uk.

things because we need to remember that God is God, and we aren't. Just like when we say "I love you" to someone, we're also saying "I don't want to be without you," so when we praise and thank God, we're reminding ourselves that we're in a relationship which needs work to be maintained; not because God will let it go, but because we, like all humans, might well take it for granted. Religious traditions (such as morning prayer, compline, mass, etc.) aren't a requirement from God to keep God happy and engaged, but to help us stay connected with that part of us which isn't visible, doesn't send monthly statements or text messages, and doesn't demand anything more of us than we wish freely to give.

When Jesus said, "The sabbath was made for humanity, not humanity for the sabbath" (Mk. 2:27 my translation), I believe he was saying that the third commandment "to remember the sabbath day and keep it holy" (Ex. 20:8) is an invitation for us to ask ourselves the question, "How do I remind myself that I'm in a relationship with the Divine Other, whose day, like every other, this day is? How do I make it holy as my gift back to God, for God's gift of this day to me?"

As Fr. Robert used to say, these are "Holy Days of Opportunity." He never called them "Days of Obligation." When celebrated as such, the communal remembering of the act Jesus asked us to do (variously called Eucharist or the Lord's Supper) is an amazing gift at the center of our being as Christians.

Personal confession time: I don't understand the Eucharist! I have no idea how it works. All I do know is that it does. I'm in relationship with this man called Jesus of Nazareth and he said we should trust him and do it, so I do. In that moment of remembering the relationship (in liturgical terms, the anamnesis), we're more open than usual to being inspired to change. And *that* is the work we're about in church; creating the space and moment into which an individual might release themselves to be met by the One who first loved them into being. As ministers we do that work of facilitating the space and moment, and then we must get out of the way, just like a good friend would know when to leave two lovers to sit on a bench at sunset and have their silent time together. Liturgical ministers should not be lemons or spare wheels in the relationships between any individual and their experience of the Divine and are most certainly not needed as a full time intermediary.

THE RELATIONSHIP BETWEEN MINISTER AND CONGREGATION

I believe that when we see the work of the liturgical presider and preacher in this light, the fact becomes clearer that it is "not just about me." This is unfortunately the opposite of what some clergy do actually seem to think, judging by their actions, (and what many were taught in some seminaries). This is particularly true if they understand what is taught as the "ontological change" of ordination is meant in a way that sets them apart and special in an inappropriate way. In the theater when we see someone taking this approach we talk about being "able to see the acting." Indeed, to be the lead actor and undertake the responsibility of that is difficult while also remaining humble and aware the effort is not just about me. This answer from Jesuit priest Richard Malloy to the question "Can you explain what happens at ordination when the 'ontological change' happens" is very helpful:

> *No! (LOL). If I could explain it, it wouldn't be what it is! Seriously, "ontological change" is very meaningful in the context of St. Thomas Aquinas' medieval theological synthesis of Aristotelian philosophy and Christian theology, a stunning intellectual achievement for both his time and, to some degree, ours.*
>
> *But once we move out of the Thomistic formulation of questions and the meaning of words in his system, we can find it more than difficult to explain what he meant then, and what it means for us now. Terms like "ontological change"... need updating for the 21st century. Jesuit Bernard Lonergan's work is a great place to start with that task. Yet, I fear most will find Lonergan quite deep and difficult. One Jesuit once said to me..."Lonergan? Life is just too short!"*
>
> *So, what does the idea of "ontological change" try to express?... Holy Orders places one in another position (i.e., order or group) in the community, not a better or more privileged place, but a place from which one is called to spend one's life exclusively in service of the people of God.*
>
> *... All of us who have been graced to serve the people of God as priests know there is often much more going on in a pastoral situation than we can understand or for which we can take credit. Someone comes up after a homily and tells you that your words were just what they needed to hear. And you realize you don't think you said what they heard... but, hey the Holy Spirit works in ways wonderful and wacky....*

> *Whatever happens on the day of ordination, I always remember what we were told by a wise, old Jesuit: "If you're not a priest the day before ordination, you won't be the day after." Ordination recognizes and brings to fruition a process that has been going on for some time in a person's life. That growth in listening to God and the people of God, while trying to facilitate conversations between God and people, continues all the days of a priest's life.*[2]

Of course, the same is true in the performing arts. Getting cast as a lead brings all sorts of extra pressure and expectations, but frequently also extra attention, kudos, and praise for anything that goes well. If you've ever waited at a stage door after a show and seen the way fans will totally ignore the other people coming out from a production until *their* favorite peeks through, such behavior can be a salutary lesson. Some actors, like clergy, do think the adulation is all about them, but in the twenty-first century any diva or divo who puts themselves on a pedestal will soon find it's a dangerous place to be. History, if not beaten to the punch by social media, will have its own critique on them.

Similarly, to bring this idea into the lives of more people than just clergy and lead actors, one can apply the words of Fr. Malloy's "wise, old Jesuit" to many other situations, for example when preparing couples for marriage. If the couple isn't married in their hearts and minds the day before the wedding, they most certainly won't be the day after, no matter how much the day costs, who says any prayers, and who ratifies the marriage license.

On the other hand, we can't ignore the fact that a person who has prepared for and lived the life of a minister or spouse (or "working actor in a lead role," as they say at the Tony and Oscar Awards) over time will be a different person from the one they were on their first day. The same is true for teachers, nurses, doctors, welders, car mechanics, seamstresses, and every other profession and skill. Experience seeps into our bones and very being so that we all can seem as if we're better than our peers in certain circumstances. Sometimes we are, when we're lucky or have more experience or just get it right. But I believe we all know that carrying the position and skill level of a proficient expert is ultimately an invitation to greater humility and understanding for others, because at this level we are also always teachers.

---

2. From Busted Halo website and blog January 12, 2010.https://bustedhalo.com/questionbox/can-you-explain-what-happens-at-ordination-when-the-ontological-change-happens.

We can also come across as self-centered, though even then we can be teachers, just of what *not* to do, and how not to do it. One of the best ways to avoid being the epitome of the latter is (a) recognize you're there to serve the people and (b) recognize and be grateful for your colleagues.

WORKS AND PLAYS WELL WITH OTHERS

Again, there can be vastly different ways to do this if one is more introverted or extroverted by nature. While the former will first want to think through how each person on the team might evaluate them and sense whether they have a relationship or not, the more extroverted will just work on the assumption that reaching out can only end well, until it doesn't.

Similarly, on the receiving end, a more introverted colleague might be stressed by an unexpected level of camaraderie, while a more extroverted one might sense one is uptight for not wanting to go to karaoke after just a couple of encounters.

In the same way, some people think that home and work lives should be kept a million miles apart, and one does not bring the personal into the workspace, and vice versa. Others work on the assumption that we only have 24 hours each day and we should fill them as best we can with as much fun, joy, and connection as they can hold, because tomorrow isn't guaranteed.

Despite these real complications, in both the church and the theater, I can't stress enough how important finding majorly significant ways to value the whole team is. We must remember and engage those who share the performance or sanctuary space, as well as those who are off-stage but still vital. We have to remember those who the audience/congregation never sees, including those who care for the space when the public work is not happening (janitors, etc.), as well as those who run the administration for the space, such as office and accounts staff. How many churches/theater companies do you know that list *all* these essential members of the whole team in the Sunday program or church website every week? More and more communities do, which is great to see.

In terms of those who share the event space, one theater exercise might be very helpful; we'll look at the topic this addresses more closely in the next chapter. The exercise is to have the cast walk through the play, not bothering much about the words but just doing the movements, and to pass a ball between them for where they think the attention or focus is at each line/speech. Usually, of course, the person speaking is the main focus, so the exercise is not complicated. However, at each ball pass, each character must answer the question: "Am I helping to direct the focus of the audience to where the production wants it or not?" Again, the question isn't too hard most of the time because if I'm not speaking, I'm most certainly not moving or doing anything to draw attention away from where it is needed. If I need to be somewhere else by the time I next speak, that's when the cast and director must work out how that happens without taking away the focus.

I believe the same rule should apply to church services. Directing the focus is so much easier in that case because, while a play doesn't usually want to stop for even a couple of seconds while someone walks from one side of the stage to the other, in church services we have no need to maintain an uninterrupted flow of words. In church we can take time. Indeed, if a person is going to speak once they've arrived at the new spot, then the walk over there is a great way to catch and guide the congregation's attention to them.

And before you say "well, that's obvious," how many times have you seen a presider fidget with a robe or book, check their watch, or give an instruction to an altar server when they aren't the focus of the moment? How many times have musicians, in full view of the congregation, discussed page numbers and song tempi while something else was happening? While such distraction won't necessarily ruin the service, it's remarkably disrespectful, and that for me is an even more important issue. When a minister, like an actor, is disrespectful of the event, the whole experience suffers. It usually means the event was not sufficiently rehearsed.

At the Roman Catholic church where I interned and then worked in Oakland, California, for six years, the space had been re-ordered (the church word for "redesigned") so that whoever was standing had the automatic focus of the congregation, be it the presider, cantor, lector/reader, preacher, or those bringing up the offerings. Whoever was standing could (a) be seen from every seat and (b) was the only person (or group of people) at least a head in height above everyone else. The reason this was done was to respect the ministry and the work of each person on the liturgical team and direct the congregation's attention. This was immensely popular with the parish, with whom the pastor (Fr. Robert, mentioned earlier) had been working for years, giving classes on church history, architecture, and liturgy. The reordering was not just a series of physical changes out of nowhere but grew out of a long-term commitment to teaching and walking with a community where he was certainly the leader but also a co-worker. This integration with the community was great modeling for a student.

Building a team, be it for a church or theater company, takes a commitment of time and energy, and a clarity of purpose. Many individuals don't want to do the work needed to build that team, preferring to bring people on board as temporary workers (paid or volunteer) who can be hired and fired at will. Holding in balance the roles of leader and co-worker is also very difficult. Even being a clear and hopefully good leader doesn't mean people won't disagree. As much as one might want to work towards decisions always being made by consensus, such cohesion is not always possible. The adage "everyone gets a voice, but not necessarily a vote" comes to mind.

In this regard I am also reminded of the wisdom from the *I Ching* of Lao Tzu:

> *A leader is best when the people hardly know he exists.*
> *When his work is done, his aim fulfilled,*
> *They will say "we did it ourselves."*

This "we" is everyone involved with a liturgical or dramatic production. Some will be more obviously involved, others less so. Some will be present at the time, others not. Some will have been paid to be there, others will pay. Some are professionals, others are volunteers.

Whenever the leaders separate themselves from the people, the whole experience of the play or worship is lessened because the relationship has been ruptured. When this happens, the words lose some or all of their communicating and transforming power. They are not made flesh as fully as they might be.

QUESTIONS FOR REFLECTION

1. The word "minister" means one who performs a service for the benefit of others. What do you really think about the people you serve? How does that affect your ministry?

2. Do you periodically get honest feedback from peers, parishioners, and friends about your ministry, including on the topic of your relationship with your community? Do you take regular classes and workshops to improve your skill level?

3. What are the non-financial gifts of affirmation, trust, etc., which you receive from your congregation?

8

Tech Week
Set Design, Music, Lighting, Sound, Costumes

The script is only a starting point, never an ending point.

WHILE ACTORS HOPE TO be able to rehearse in a space that at least resembles the final performance space, with doors and stairs in the correct position, that isn't always possible. Church ministers are luckier in that regard as their space is, on average, largely unused for most of the week. (Why seems a great question, but for another time.)

Actors are sometimes not in their final space until a week before opening night, for what's formally known in that trade as Tech Week but more informally as Hell Week. This is when all the other functions needed for the final production, and which have been working away in their own workshops and offices, are brought together if they haven't been already added to the rehearsals. And there are often a lot of surprises. The stairs and doorways are now fixed, though may need to be negotiated with new clothes which, if you're suddenly wearing a period costume or just a long skirt, might prove more constraining than previously realized. Probably the worst "surprise!!" is to find that no one mentioned that the stage has a serious rake, the sometimes very steep slope built into older theaters so that actors towards the back could be seen from an audience who were all on a level floor.

Similarly, the lighting design will now be implemented, and suddenly you can't see when you look from the stage because you're blinded by a light directly in your eyes. The effect is delightful for the audience, maybe with dappled leaves from the supposed tree outside the window dancing across your face, but you now can't find the chair you're meant to sit in because the stage is all a blur. Hopefully you have a couple of minutes to recover before you must move again. This all has to be negotiated and worked through.

In a musical, shifting from a rehearsal pianist to a full band or orchestra adds its own issues, especially if a note you're used to hearing on the piano is now coming from a trumpet. Ah, the joys of live theater! And that's why it's called "Hell Week," because, whatever happens or fails to happen, the clock is ticking and come opening night, the show must go on.

Despite all these potential drawbacks, theater wouldn't be the same without having all these wonderful options, even if they're limited by the budget and the collective imagination.

Looking back a few hundred years, Shakespeare and his colleagues didn't have much by way of these choices. If you've ever been to a reconstructed outdoor Elizabethan theater, you'll know that the architecture was pretty set, with a stage, some supporting columns for the balcony, and three entrances and exits. It was painted in the decorous style of the early Renaissance and, apart from the addition of a few moveable set pieces (chairs, benches, etc.) and props, and maybe a drape or flag or two, that was it. Performances were given during the daylight because candles weren't powerful enough for large groups at night, and larger naked flames too dangerous, especially for anyone wearing a long flowing costume. One penny was charged to stand in the pit for a three- or four-hour production, and more to sit on the benches which went up three galleries high behind the pit. Cushions were an extra charge. Speaking of costumes, they were largely based on the clothes of the period, with adaptations for what passed for "other countries" if an Arab or African outfit were needed. And don't forget that all the female parts were played by young men and boys, women being prohibited from appearing on stage as such exposure was considered too risqué.

When we compare the theater and the church of this period, the parallel is remarkably strong. Churches had very defined and limited style and architecture during the European late Medieval period and early Renaissance. As their locations changed from village to city, from chapel to cathedral, more windows with glass (one of the best inventions of the tenth and eleventh centuries) and taller arches and spires were added. This architecture reflected the theology and the sociology of the day. A unity was present in the arts (and particularly architecture) and theology right through the Reformation, for God was big and grand and "up there," and so therefore was the church building. They reflected the Divine's power and status. The House of God, no longer representing the domestic *domus ecclesiae* (the home of the community), was always the tallest building in the neighborhood, and frequently had the largest footprint too, though homes for the wealthy and titled did get much bigger around then.

In the UK, where in the fifteenth and sixteenth centuries Anglicanism more or less took over all the buildings that were once Catholic, the physical changes were not too marked, except in a simplification of the vesture of clergy and reduction in the other images allowed in churches. (The United Kingdom was to go through its own second reformation a little later, with the Civil War and the rise of Oliver Cromwell and the Puritans, *et al.*, in the seventeenth century. As those who have read their history know, this second reformation was much more destructive to buildings and ordinary people.) Most northern European countries, however, similarly engaged in the Reformation, saw a remarkable shift to simplicity much earlier, with the whitewashing of ancient frescos, the breaking of stained-glass windows, and the smashing of all statues. The Quakers, while not so destructive, were famous for their simple spaces, which was even reflected in the design of their chairs, benches, and clothes. Southern Europe remained mainly Catholic.

In more Puritan cultures, acting and dancing were banned for good measure too. Officially sanctioned joy was to be found in very limited places. (We are back to a strong separation between Apollo and Dionysus.) God may not have been reduced in power, but the human edifices created and decorated in that name frequently were, as were ideas of what was meant by being created in that Divine image. (Maybe this was the beginning of the war on play?)

Things didn't change much for a couple of hundred years after that. Where the theology was more Catholic the culture tended to be more catholic, with life and art, both good and bad, flourishing and playing an active role in society. Where more "reformed" minds were in charge, social life was more limited. This is most clear with the communal developments in the new colonies of what was to become America, where various European influences (England and France particularly, but also the Dutch and Germanic cultures, followed by the Italians, Spanish, and more recently Asians) have all contributed to both the Catholic and Puritan ends of the spectrum, alongside locally grown theologies of self-improvement and spiritual enlightenment. (To name a few: the American Baptist Church [1638], Mormonism [1820s], Seventh Day Adventists [1830s], and Church of Christ, Scientist [1879]). The architectural styles of these various denominations are worth exploring for unique features which reflect their different theologies as well as similarities, which speaks to a somewhat limited vocabulary for imagining the sacred in three-dimensional space.

The theological developments that have become more mainstream since World War Two have had little effect on church architecture largely because (a) for most people the changes are relatively minor and (b) no one has the money to knock down existing buildings and rebuild for the new community. (This latter point might actually be good news for architectural preservationists, even though the buildings no longer match the theology of the current occupants.) Post World War Two damaged areas did see new buildings, but many reverted to rebuilding old structures rather than finding new shapes and materials. The arrival of "storefront churches" is new, as has been churches moving into industrial areas, where they'll use a building initially designed as a warehouse or some such and then renovate on the inside. These can make great sound studios and places for effective lighting, but often have no natural light or windows. They are very functional but rarely inspiring, which is certainly not my idea of what best exemplifies the Divine Other. But then, it's not all about God, is it? Or me.

Old churches are, on the other hand, great for creating a sense of longevity and consistency, for having an atmosphere conducive to prayer and reflection, with wonderful acoustics for music. However, most even medium sized ones are very poor at delivering the spoken word or providing good sightlines, enabling everyone to feel connected and involved, and very hard to adapt to different seasons or events. Rather than the theater's raked stage to aid viewability, most older churches go for steps and levels, making the altar and pulpit higher. Only recently have churches been built with the altar on the floor and the seating tiered around it, like an old Roman amphitheater. In some ways, history might be thought to have had the last laugh.

Theater spaces have changed in a similar way over this period, with old buildings slowly being adapted to the (expensive) new technologies, and microphones being used to boost the natural voices of actors and singers, enabling them among other things to turn their backs on the audience and still be heard. This is a huge improvement because in most theaters built between 1500 and 1940, if you didn't speak directly out to the audience, they couldn't hear you. All the amazing work done by ancient Roman and Greek builders had been forgotten, thought "old-fashioned" or impractical in localities of cooler climes. Mediterranean ancients didn't worry about putting a roof over their spaces, something that would be very limiting much further north, although their ruins do exist. This ancient styling can be found in some modern structures built on the old amphitheater model though usually, because of drapes and sets, they lack the hard, flat surface needed to bounce the sound forward. Modern audiences tend to want carpets and soft seats, which absorb the sounds significantly. However, the viewability is excellent.

The good news about technological advances is that the possibility of what a set can look like these days is beyond amazing. One group of leaders in this has been the teams who have worked in the late twentieth century on musicals, particularly those of composer Andrew Lloyd Webber. While critics have not always loved the melodies (though audiences are frequently greatly enamored by them), the innovations in set design and technology which Webber's money and commitment to perfection (at least as he sees it, and he's usually his own producer) has made possible have been remarkable. Millions of people worldwide have seen *Phantom of the Opera,* with a boat that glides over the stage, and candelabra that come up from within it, not to mention a giant chandelier that flies in and out! Add to that the entire second stage that floats above the main stage in *Sunset Boulevard* so that two scenes can happen simultaneously. Or how about the four-lane highway that slides onto the set fifteen feet above the stage for his adaptation of *Whistle down the Wind*? And who will ever forget a rollerblade racetrack that rose to the second tier above the audience for *Starlight Express,* or a helicopter landing and taking off from the stage in *Miss Saigon* (not in this case by Webber, but with music by Claude-Michel Schönberg and Alain Boublil, and lyrics by Boublil and Richard Maltby Jr.)? Not me!

Were all these shows masterpieces? Maybe not. Were they remarkably popular? Absolutely yes! (Except possibly *Whistle down the Wind.*) Did someone spend the time and energy (and, yes, money) to ensure the set was everything the work needed to succeed as best it could? I would have to say, yes indeed. Were the solutions with which we are now familiar the only solutions? No, simpler and/or less expensive ones might have been considered which would have worked just as effectively. But by bringing these shows (and many, many others) to reality in the way they were added a dimension which shifted the possibility for theater into the future. And they taught an amazing lesson about commitment to the entirety and integrity of a piece.

Alongside this truth, some accuse Lloyd Webber and others of relying on spectacle and expensive gimmicks to carry a piece when others rely on their writing and the casts' acting and singing skills to do that work. Many a great show has succeeded with much less to support it. One thinks of Stephen Sondheim's *Company*, for example, or the 1996 pared-down production of *Chicago* staged and choreographed by Bob Fosse. And then in even more contemporary masterpieces such as *Hamilton*, *Wicked*, and *The Lion King* skillful staging doesn't always rely on excessively expensive productions.

So, what does this tell us? I would suggest three takeaways of the many available:

- People enjoy strong production values (and yes, gimmicks) *as long as* a similar amount of good content is evident.
- To find a piece that has a universal appeal to large audience numbers as well as professional critics is rare yet also wonderful.
- Not creating around the theme of love (usually romantic) automatically makes selling a piece to a significant part of the populace harder, though just working around love by no means predicts that a piece will be successful.

What does this tell us for church? To adapt P.T. Barnum's adage, I think we are told that you can engage some of the people all the time, all the people some of the time, but not all the people all the time.

A lot of the more Evangelical, Pentecostal and Community churches (and many are very successful in terms of growing memberships) seem to follow this modern musical model, with great lighting rigs, slide shows, house bands, and yes, even smoke effects on special occasions. Worship is "of the moment," come as you are, and yes, bring your coffee too if you want.[1]

---

1. References for details about megachurches and how they are doing: https://www.npr.org/2023/07/14/1187460517/megachurches-growing-liquid-church. Also "Not who you think they are: Who goes to megachurches compared to other Protestant

When a pastor or pastoral team are trying to plant or grow a eucharistic liturgical church, the challenge to balance the tradition, or rather Tradition, with the new is huge. The question seems to be what can be done that both maintains the Tradition yet also says "this is new and fresh and engaging—please come give it a try"?

Within this challenge, one of the most difficult obstacles for many churches is the architecture, especially in older communities with older buildings, in spite of the generations of believers who have prayed there. If the space doesn't reflect the contemporary community or their theology, it adds an extra challenge to celebrating authentic contemporary liturgy there. Any visitors may also receive a conflicting message.

The Church of England's parish of St. Stephen Walbrook in the ancient City of London is a great example. The original church, built on the foundations for a temple to Mithras while the Romans were in town (47–410 CE) dates somewhere between 700 and 980 CE. Its later known manifestation (1428), about twenty feet away from the original, was burnt down in 1666's Great Fire of London. Sir Christopher Wren redesigned the church (he also lived on the same street, close to his major post-fire project, St. Paul's Cathedral), and the church was ready for use by 1673 (meaning 2023 was the 350th anniversary of the "new" building). It was next damaged during the London Blitz in the Second World War, and languished post-war in a sad state. It was brought back to life as London was rebuilt but faced the same fate as many inner-city Christian parishes in the 1960s, with falling attendance and activity. Facing this reality, the vestry (parish council) decided to refocus the work of the parish and develop new outreach ministries for when people were around—basically Monday through Friday. It's closed on most Saturdays and Sundays. To reflect this new focus, they decided to take the bold step and reorder the whole space, which included commissioning a new altar for the center of the church by the very modern (at the time) sculptor Henry Moore, using travertine marble from the same quarry as that used by Michelangelo.

The new work caused them to review their space, and this new altar piece transformed both the building and, in turn, the community who chose to gather. As the church says on its website: "If you want to know what a community believe see how they worship."[2]

---

churches 2008 research." https://www.christianpost.com/news/survey-examines-america-s-megachurchgoers.html.

2. The church's website has a very interesting story about the rebuilding of the space and the thought that went into it, including reflecting biblical symbolism and the need

If you think "old" and "new" cannot co-exist, I invite you to view a service from St. Stephen's, their website has a link.³

Often older communities say they can't change the interior of their worship spaces. However, unless the interior space is on a list for historical protection, that isn't true. They can; they just don't want to, or do want to, but lack the financial resources. As in the case of St. Stephen's, even when elements of the interior are listed, what is essential can be retained, just re-purposed.

When I hear arguments for maintaining "we've always done it this way" without any further discussion, what I hear is primarily an unwillingness to re-evaluate the reasons for the original decisions which gave a community this reality. If, upon reevaluation, the current space perfectly represents everything the community wants to say about itself and its theology, change is not needed, and to do so would be a form of sacrilege. However, I believe that the appeal to unquestioned tradition is frequently one of several other things, including:

- An excuse for laziness
- The coziness of monotony
- A fear of change, a subjective "if it ain't broke, don't fix it" attitude.
- A lack of imagination, and fear of reaching out to others who might have that imagination
- Believing you don't have permission to have an opinion
- A fear of being wrong
- A fear of the cost, financially as well as in membership

Rarely does a good excuse exist for change for change's sake, but similarly no good reason exists for the opposite either. When examining the adage "If you continue doing what you've always done, you're going to get what you've always got," for most contemporary parishes that means shrinking numbers and an ever-aging population. The problem is that these questions become more urgent with each passing year.

The benefits of a modern arena-styled theater, (for example the Littleton Theatre inside London's National Theatre complex or the Peter Jay Sharp Theatre in the Lincoln Center in new York), are that one can change the feel of the space with each production—a proscenium stage

---

to be a church for contemporary Christians. https://ststephenwalbrook.net.

3. Here's one from 2023. https://www.youtube.com/watch?v=mMthSlL4bwY.

for one show, an open thrust for the next, and a combination of both with a sunken orchestra pit in between for the next. One can have a full, realistic set with walls and working appliances for one show, while another can contain just token elements, and a third be completely monochrome. Because a theater is basically a black box, it can become anything the team wishes it to become, within the limits of creativity and money. And of course, we have Shakespeare's great solution when money and space are short, as found at the beginning of his spectacular play *Henry V*, when he invites the audience to use its imagination to fill in the gaps:

> *O, for a muse of fire that would ascend*
> *The brightest heaven of invention!*
> *A kingdom for a stage, princes to act,*
> *And monarchs to behold the swelling scene!*
> *Then should the warlike Harry, like himself,*
> *Assume the port of Mars, and at his heels,*
> *Leashed in like hounds, should famine, sword, and fire*
> *Crouch for employment. But pardon, gentles all,*
> *The flat unraisèd spirits that hath dared*
> *On this unworthy scaffold to bring forth*
> *So great an object. Can this cockpit hold*
> *The vasty fields of France? Or may we cram*
> *Within this wooden O the very casques*
> *That did affright the air at Agincourt?*

To hear a preacher invite the congregation to engage their imagination is rare, but I've witnessed it being done very effectively and memorably! Theater is, after all, largely based on the unspoken contract between cast and audience for a common suspended belief. When an actor says they're on a raft in a storm-tossed sea, we believe them, even though we know we're all on dry land. This is basically the same as when a child decides their bed is a spacecraft and the pillows are laser-proof shields against enemy death rays. When an actor dies on stage, we cry, as if they were indeed dead, even though we know they'll be up and taking a bow to great applause in about three minutes.

When we go to a live performance, we expect to engage our imagination. If not, we would consider a play the same thing as a lecture, and prepare to take notes rather than be transported. A theater audience will be trusted to fill in the gaps as needed, with the production providing just enough support to keep them moving in the desired direction. This is partly why every production always guarantees the "full, active and conscious participation" of the audience even though they are not singing along with the tunes or answering questions from the stage.[4] Even without a set change, a small costume change can take us from 1890 to 1990 in a moment, a lighting one can move us from midday to midnight in this same moment. All these functions and skill sets work together to guide the audience in its role as the receiver of the play, and the play exists in their imaginations and memories, nowhere else.

The audience gets to take home the play when they leave. The actors' and production team's jobs are to help it survive the journey home and to last for as long as the audience members want to make it last. Each audience member might remember different parts in different ways. This is fine, for the reality is that the audience hasn't experienced just one play. Though only one script and one production is presented, as many versions of the play are perceived as the number of people who've seen it enfleshed and presented for consumption, to nourish and enlighten them, to inform and entertain them. Every preacher knows this too, when different congregants hear something different yet you only gave one homily or sermon.

Theater companies spend a lot of time and resources costuming and lighting a show and creating sets to develop the sense of a cohesive whole, which helps the audience to engage with the production and the script. For a children's fairytale or pantomime, one might want to overemphasize the visual elements with bright colors and sparkle, while for a production of *The Miracle Worker*[5], aimed at a similar age group, one would usually take a very different route. Yet if this difference is obvious in the theater, it appears less so in the church.

Variations in music in church, of course, have been accepted for centuries, and have become more diverse in the past seventy years. Openness to other changes is more recent, especially the idea that a church environment can make a positive contribution to the liturgy, and not just add decoration. I remember the first time I saw something that seemed to bring new meaning to a church season, and that was Christmas of

---

4. This target of "full, active and conscious participation" is one of the hallmarks of contemporary liturgical planning, drawn from Vatican II's Sacrosanctum Concilium (the liturgy document) as well as the aforementioned document *Lumen Gentium*, but in parishes it is too often reduced to externals and not so much concerned with internal engagement as a play is.

5. *The Miracle Worker* is a play by William Gibson based on Helen Keller's autobiography *The Story of my Life*.

1990, during the First Gulf War and Operation Desert Storm. The family responsible for creating the Nativity manger scene that year for the local Catholic parish I attended in Forest Hill, London, (St. William of York) decided to set it on sand, not straw, and created a backdrop which subtly reflected the war situation. Such presentation was a revelation to many of us, including the clergy.

CREATING LITURGICAL SPACES THAT ENGAGE THE IMAGINATION AND THE LIMINAL

A few years later, I took the same idea to the church where I was an intern lay minister, St. Paschal Baylon in Oakland, California, under Fr. Robert. On Christmas Eve a friend and I created a makeshift stable for the Holy Family and plastered it with roughly torn extracts from newspapers of that week concerning war, AIDS, homelessness and corruption. Over this we painted the words "Love," "Peace," and "Joy" in gold, with (battery-charged) candles under each. Over the barn we placed the large Good Friday cross, casting its shadow. The pastor came to see it, stood in silence for a while, and then went back to his office and re-wrote his homily for that night, newly themed about our life as the stories in a newspaper, and how Jesus comes as the Good News, a Word made flesh for today.

One of the things I've learned over the years is that preaching on the big feasts is harder because everyone basically knows what you're going to say, and the story has a difficult time developing. Also, the "Christmas and Easter crowd" who attend only those events, but in significant numbers, are largely un-churched and coming from a different place than the regulars. This means that the addition of something like a different creche each year can help everyone engage, including the preacher.

From this simple start we decided to look at the major seasons coming up, such as Lent, Easter, and then Pentecost. Following a review of the gospels for the Great Ninety Days that year, we decided to treat them as a single journey in three acts, where one set of environmental changes led into the next. Consequently, instead of our usual large Lenten cross hanging above the altar, that year saw a ten-yard piece of heavy gauge rope hung, loosely looped in an off-center knot, with the cross off to one side. At the first service of that first Lenten weekend, one of the old-timers arrived and, meeting the pastor at the back of the church, asked, "What's that?" Catching on to the work, Fr. Robert replied, "What do you think it is?" After a moment, the parishioner replied, "Well, it could be our bondage to sin. It could be the rope that Judas used to hang himself. Hmm, I think I'm getting the idea of this," and walked to his seat. The imagination had been engaged, and he was free to take that in any direction he wanted, or wherever the Spirit might lead.

This showed us that the work had begun to take root. People were being invited to engage with their worship using more of themselves than just their ears and voices, and they weren't running away screaming! They were invited, stimulated by visual prompts, to use their imagination, and to engage at a deeper level. Importantly, we didn't ask anyone to "talk about it" unless they brought it up, although some certainly did. Though putting it like this might sound somewhat grandiose, the work was an attempt by the environment team to set up a visual openness to vulnerability between the individual and the Divine. Our job wasn't to direct this, just to work to enable it, whatever "it" turned out to be, and then trust the process.

We were lucky to have a very neutral liturgical space, which had started as a gymnasium and was now a church. By the time we got through that Pentecost, we were regularly being asked, "What are you going to do next year?" and the new untraditional tradition was started.

Following the same process, another year the readings for the First Sunday of Lent started with the story of Noah's Ark, the flood, and the appearance of the rainbow. For those unfamiliar with liturgical churches, Lent is usually a time when we explore the desert, a waterless symbol of the Jewish story of wandering after leaving Egypt. No flowers are in the space, the font is usually drained, and the general feel is about absence. This of course all gets turned around at the Easter Vigil when we celebrate baptisms (and in this church they were able to celebrate these in an immersion font). Genesis 9:8–15 picks up the story just as God is promising not to send another flood, and to place a rainbow in the heavens as a sign of the new covenant. We decided therefore that, while the rainbow would arrive at Easter, for Lent we would explore what living in a flood, not a desert, was like.

The music team found great songs and hymns which reflected this, and the environment team came up with something that shocked everyone: we decided to (figuratively) flood the congregation and the whole space over the first five weeks of Lent, covering even the stations of the cross. If spiritual metanoia is truly about turning around, then we have to be willing to let everything go in order to be free. When someone suffers a flood, they can literally see their life being swept away, including all the old ways. That includes even the old traditions and comforts. We knew letting go was a risk but, hey, the ordeal would be over in six weeks, so what's the worst that could happen? We had promised them a beautiful Easter and Christmas; but Lent and Advent was when we asked the community to let us challenge them.

The idea was to explore the question "what has to be let go of in the water?" We did it by painting eight large panels (two for each wall) on gray paper, about nine by twelve feet (three by four meters) when fully unfurled. (This was available from a photography supply store, the sort photographers use for backdrops.) Using black, magenta, and purple paints in very broad, dramatic, and abstract strokes, we painted them as if Jackson Pollock and Franz Kline had had a paint-off. The panels were each hung on a twelve-foot rod, and the hanging rope, which we dyed purple, went from the ends of the rods up to the ceiling, and then back down to cinder blocks on the floor. The first week the rods were hung so that most of each painting was rolled up on the floor, with just the top three feet revealed. Each week the cinder blocks were turned, wrapping the rope around them so that the rods were raised, revealing more and more of the paintings, passing over the stations of the cross on week four and at full extension by Palm Sunday, for which occasion we added splashes of red paint.

As you might imagine, not everyone liked it or initially approved. However, the pastor stuck with us and reminded everyone that the sun would be returning at Easter, with a rainbow, and kept inviting everyone to ask themselves the question of "what needs to be left in the water?" This echoed one of the questions we asked parents or catechumens when they came or brought children for baptism.

When the final Palm Sunday mass was over, one of the long-time regulars asked me to meet her by her seat in the church. She didn't look happy. What she wanted to tell me was something like this: "I've sat here for six weeks looking at this thing creep up the wall. I've always supported you and the artistic work you've done here, but this time I'm afraid I thought you'd completely lost it. It's ugly. It distracted me, and I didn't get it. But Fr Robert's question kept ringing in my ears. And then this week I realized." At this point she turned to the now-huge painting closest to her and started pointing to different places and saying things like: "This is where my mother died. That is where my sister got diagnosed with cancer. This is where a friend was killed in Vietnam. And now I can let the pain of those memories go and you can take this down and burn it." And that's exactly what we did; we tore a piece from each painting and used them to light the Easter Fire.

If I were ever to do this again, I would invite the parishioners to write or draw on the paintings, adding their words for what they wanted to be left in the flood water. The process had taken the whole journey of Lent, but this risk of challenging a congregation to engage with their own prayers, fears, and sorrows in the communal space helped at least one person pray and then accept the healing they had long sought. I didn't get fired, so maybe a few others got it too. Who knows?

One important note to make here is that at no point in this celebration of Lent did we change anything about the official script. We didn't make the whole thing about the paintings; they were just there as the visual context for what would've happened anyway. Yes, we took every opportunity to make appropriate links, as one always does, with hymns, other music, and prayers which can be adapted. The purpose of sharing this story is to say that when we take the opportunity to go outside the traditional way of contextualizing what we do in church, we can unlock new experiences using the other senses than just hearing and the intellect, primarily the imagination.

When the congregation returned on Easter Sunday, eight other paintings were in the space, this time on yellow paper hanging from the ceiling, again all done by parishioners on very inexpensive paper from the photography suppliers. Each showed a waterfall splashing down into an array of flowers in every color of the rainbow. Water was no longer deadly but life-giving. To finish off the transition from Lent to Easter, we commissioned (again from parishioner volunteers) a new white chasuble, lined with yellow (to match the paper of the paintings). Over one shoulder flowed the painted image of another small waterfall which was matched with a new very large alter cloth, in basic white, but with similarly painted streams flowing down each corner and then "pooling" at the floor to reference the Book of Revelation's streams of living water going out from the throne of the Lamb in the new Jerusalem. And to end the ninety days, for Pentecost the descending water became descending flames.[6]

6. Other ideas we worked with included the Lent-Easter-Pentecost time as a journey. The chosen people of the Jewish scriptures traveled in the desert for forty years, which reflects Lent's forty days. Then the early new Christian community first gathered and celebrated the Resurrection and was, at Pentecost, sent out to proclaim the Good News. This became visualized by us as the Tent of Journey (Lent), the Marque of Celebration (Easter), and the Big Top of Traveling Good News (Pentecost). And yes, we did

When the final Sunday of that liturgical year (the Feast of Christ the King) came around, we decided to bring out elements of everything we had used from Advent onwards. Always a popular time for adding visuals, as it is (in America at least) near Thanksgiving and various harvest festivals, this year the church space was particularly full, focused not just around the altar but, as we always tried, into the corners of the basically square space so that elements were always close to the people, and no one was far from something. That Sunday we truly celebrated abundance! But the real reason for doing this was that the next Sunday was the beginning of a new liturgical year. To celebrate the First Sunday of Advent *everything* extra was removed, and the space was returned to an amazing stark simplicity to emphasize the new season and its meaning. This was an example of how artists use "negative space" (the visual equivalent of silence and stillness) as much as positive space to create an artwork. To create emptiness, one has to have an experience of fullness; to create newness, one has to be aware of oldness. This is about more than just "change;" this is about stimulating and enabling conscious transition.

FINDING THE COURAGE TO LIVE IN THE NOW AND THE NEW

One of the important elements of the difference between one thing being a decoration and another being an engaging installation or environmental art piece can be scale. Neither the scripts of the stage nor the church are presented without consideration for this. In the theater this is usually done very consciously. In the church such presentation is usually completely unconscious because "this is the building we've got; it's been this way for years," or maybe centuries. Plus, of course, the ubiquitous opinion "the people wouldn't like it being messed around with" rears its head. Most church leaders aren't trained even to ask the question "what else can help us here?" let alone explore outside the traditional box containing music and flowers. On the other hand, all theater directors, (and apparently most megachurch pastors,) are always looking at as many avenues as possible to ensure the script will reach its final destination.

Often the building we call "church" can be a limitation, not an aid to the work. I've known many ministers who have rejoiced when their

---

actually build and adapt over the ninety days three tent-like structures which covered a significant amount of the space and congregation, centered above the altar.

building was unusable for some reason—one once lost theirs permanently in an earthquake, another temporarily for a roofing issue. Moving into a large tent or the church hall became an opportunity to sidestep the old ways and seek out the new.

Just as with a theater script, no elements of the official script needed to be changed or removed, which would be a step too far for some denominations. This type of work should probably be called liturgical installations because the work is not about ancillary decoration but creating a new sense of space, a new "somewhere" we're inviting people to place their body and take their breath. People are invited, temporarily, one season at a time, to live inside the experience created. The purpose is to support the work of the script in communicating with the congregation, and doing that year after year, decade after decade. At any age, people can be very grateful for new lenses on old stories. We've heard them so many times before, we're in danger of falling foul of the old adage "familiarity breeds contempt." And, as when a piece of theater has no set or costumes it's called a "staged reading," when the set and costumes are missing in church the message is that the communication is relying for its effectiveness on less than the total number of channels available. This is fine for a preview, as for a new work, or to try and get the feel for a classic that's not possible to stage fully; but such offering is not theater at its best, and it's not church at its fullest potential either. A big difference exists between consciously designed minimalism and not trying.

Traditionally there are seven well-documented ways in which people process information, learn and communicate:

- Visual
- Auditory
- Reading and Writing
- Kinesthetic
- Logical & Analytical
- Social & Interpersonal
- Solitary & Intrapersonal

How many of these modes of proclaiming the Good News does your team engage across all age ranges? While we all have our preferred modes, a ministerial team (even if that's just you) needs to find ways to access some of the other six.

QUESTIONS FOR REFLECTION

1. As the director of your Sunday liturgical script, do you know who your colleagues and peers are in the other fields of design, music, hospitality, and communication? Are they well trained? Do you respect what they add to the services? Are you scared of competition and losing control?

2. How well do you deal with subject areas outside your area of expertise, especially creative ones?

3. As a preacher, how comfortable are you over time in using more than one of the seven learning styles in your sermon or homily? Or are you a one-track communicator?

9

Knowing and Delivering Your Lines

Take your work and commitment seriously, but never yourself.

How many times have I forgotten my lines? Often! I can honestly say as actor, presider, and preacher that I've lost my way in a script, memorized or not, on enough occasions to know I always need to have prompts hidden nearby or a "get out" strategy. And that doesn't even include having to rephrase something because I've forgotten the exact words, or realizing afterwards (usually by someone pointing it out) that I had reworded something unknowingly. Equally, on more than one occasion I hadn't realized I had forgotten a section which I had jumped right over until it was pointed out later. As a presider I've never "jumped over" the institution narrative of a eucharistic prayer, but I've been at a Sunday mass where it happened. And I've seen the equivalent happen several times on stage, to me and others, where an actor is talking away quite happily, and you realize they've jumped a whole page of dialogue and cut half your lines, including the answers to three significant questions for the plot. As comfortable as one might be with a script, mistakes can happen.

Finally, in this spirit of confession, I've even used the wrong name for someone on stage. I introduced them by my character's name instead of theirs. I corrected myself and got a laugh—luckily it was a comedy—but such lapse is never something you want to have happen, believe me.

There are clearly three main groups who are the focus of this book; those who don't learn their lines because they've been told memorization is not required, those who improvise the whole service, and those who try to learn their lines because it improves their ability to do their work. Of the "never need to bother" group, at one end we have those who always rely on the fact that they have everything written in a book, as with most liturgical presiders, along with preachers who only work from a full script. On the other end of this spectrum, we have those who sometimes or always preside and/or preach without notes, trusting their preparation process and the Holy Spirit in the moment. Considerable benefits and pitfalls attach to both approaches.

Always relying on a book means we're tempted to under-prepare, resulting in being taken by surprise by words we don't know or getting meanings wrong because of sentence construction. Also, if the order of service isn't on continuous pages in the service book, the chance of getting lost, even temporarily, looms, which I suspect we've all seen on multiple occasions. Having said that, most of the time this approach probably gives adequate renditions of the script, if not ones that bring forth anything new, engaging, or exciting. What is lacking in energy is made up for in familiarity. However, this delivery can render a script flat and uninteresting. The era of the "fourteen-minute Latin mass" may have ended (we hope), but speed reading is still a lively sport in some parishes on a Sunday. (After all, as I heard one pastor say, "We have to get folks home in time for whatever game is on TV that day.")

Alternatively, not using a script means we can truly surrender to the Holy Spirit to inspire and lead us in the moment. If one is working with a Quaker or similar community, where silence is truly valued, that can be very freeing. We can wait to be inspired and not feel any pressure to "say something important" regardless of having no clear prompt from the Spirit. However, if you have a church full of folks used to being able to get out in fifty-five minutes to get on with their weekend, or one loses one's thread and the message fails to land, or the prayer fails to make logical sense or have cohesion, then the aid of a script suddenly might seem a great relief.

I suspect we've all had moments when unscripted words flowed freely and naturally, and even we were surprised by our own wisdom and inspiration. (It wasn't probably ours, but we'll usually be happy to own it for as long as we can remember it.) If you can pull that off even most of the time, consider yourself a master of the art of preaching or presiding.

Anyone past the proverbial ten thousand hours of practice is probably there. But that doesn't mean a script doesn't have a place too.[1]

Wanting the effect of spontaneity but with the security of a prepared script, some presiders and preachers do decide to learn their words "by heart" so that they may deliver them with freedom for their eyes to engage the congregation and to be in the moment, just as actors are required to do.

Learning lines isn't easy for most of us; it takes a lot of time and practice. Plus, the possibility of getting them wrong is always lurking, even after much time and effort, so why do it if you don't have to take on that pressure? The answer usually comes with the script, and whether the minister and the situation conspire to get it right or not. By "right" I mean delivering it to the best of my ability and skill, working to create the fullest moment and meaning the script can hold. Unfortunately, some church cultures seem to suggest that "phoning it in" is sufficient. However, for most preachers and presiders, somewhere along that spectrum of skill and effort is the sustainable "sweet spot" of a person's professionalism, where relying on a script yet being open to inspiration are in balance, and we're adequately, if not inspiringly, doing the work that is our job.

In theater a definite distinction exists between a script, which has been labored over and honed to where the author feels it's finished, and an improvisation, where the actor(s), with or without significant preparation, create something in the moment. In practice, even when a person is performing their own piece, they prefer creating a script first so that they can control not only the content but also the sequence and flow of the piece. We see this a lot with the better stand-up comedians. A whole evening may seem off the cuff, working the audience, but nine times out of ten a structured and well-prepared script is behind it all which acts like the scaffolding for the time.[2]

Improvisations have a different energy than constructed pieces, and often require a different sort of performer, a quick thinker, often more

1. Malcolm Gladwell's book *Outliers: The Story of Success* suggests that this magic number of ten thousand hours of practice is what it takes to be a master at something. It has never been proved or thoroughly disproved. However, it remains a proverbial benchmark for those who are trying to better themselves in a practice or habit, symbolizing the moment when the action becomes second nature and we move into a state of being "it" not just trying to do the skill.

2. A personal favorite to see is Mike Birbiglia, who can fill a whole evening telling one story (with multiple hysterical side roads) that takes the audience on a unified yet hilarious journey. Sleepwalk with Me and My Girlfriend's Boyfriend are personal favorites. The latter show, in 2013, got a resounding 100 percent on the Rotten Tomatoes "Tomatometer." He should be required viewing for every preaching or storytelling class.

extroverted and one who gets energized by the adrenaline and the pressure of the moment.

While contemporary liturgical clergy in some traditions are used to being significantly constrained by a script, that wasn't always the case. As far back as the writing of the Didache (sometime around 100 CE) the still largely Jewish-in-style Christian communities around the Mediterranean were used to a balance of both scripted and unscripted prayers. The scripted ones included, of course, the Lord's Prayer and what we now call the institution narrative (also known as the consecration), which was to be said before the sharing of the bread and cup during a Sunday gathering or service. However, they were also accustomed to more spontaneous prayers. Guidance was given that those leading the service "should pray for" certain things but the form was left free. And while examples are sometimes given in the works of the Church Fathers of how a prayer *might* look or sound, these were not given as requirements but suggestions. After all, although these letters and books were written in one language (usually Greek or Latin), each community would be saying the prayers in their own tongue.

The standardization of what became the western Roman Catholic Church using only Latin and the eastern Orthodox Church using only Greek didn't happen until the late fourth century, when the Roman Empire Constantine had united in 325 CE and recentered from Rome to what became Constantinople was divided back into its constituent parts. Although each western (aka Latin Rite) diocese could (and did) have its own Sacramentary (the official book containing the scripts and other guidance for celebrating the sacraments), the move towards each diocese only using the one from the diocese of Rome slowly grew throughout the subsequent centuries, until it was made the official rule at the Council of Trent in the mid-sixteenth century, partly in response to the Reformation movement.

For clergy, one of the unique challenges of using a liturgical script is that, while an actor is either talking to another actor or occasionally to the audience, a liturgical presider is talking to the congregation or to God. In a sense the persons of the Trinity are the other actors in the drama of the liturgy. Christian prayers, by and large, are addressed to "The Father" (or Mother, Creator, God beyond all names, etc.), who is asked to act because the son Jesus promised us our prayers would be heard, and the power in which that action happens is through their Holy Spirit or "in Jesus' name."

For the presider, how do we shift our delivery between talking to the congregation as normal speech (as in "hello everyone, and welcome to today's service") and inviting the congregation into the "sacred moment" ("let us pray"), and then speaking to the Divine on behalf of the whole community? The answer lies with those three essentials we mentioned back in the Prologue: we need clarity about the different intentions (which isn't complicated), the different words (which are often given, so is also often easy), and the different relationships I have with each person or group involved in the dialogue. This last requirement is the one where we have challenges, because my body and hence my breath can be different, sometimes very different, as I move through the relationships.

I'm reminded of the invitation of Rev. Dr. L. William Countryman, a deservedly popular scripture professor and writer at the Episcopalian Church Divinity School of the Pacific who, at the beginning of any service, always invited us to "first remember that God is always present, so let us remind ourselves that we are in that presence now." And then he would give himself and us time to arrive there. He was asking us to remember that our "calling out to God" as if we had to attract God's attention is not a realistic understanding of our Christian theology; for God is, as various poets and writers have said, always closer to us than our breath. The issue is not about attracting the Divine's attention but focusing our own. That takes time and practice. With practice, even a deep breath will be enough.

If I hear one criticism about too many (though certainly not all) presiders, it's that they don't sound believable when they're speaking, as if they aren't invested in the words or the script. They're doing little more than just reciting the words. This can possibly be excused for some older Roman Catholic clergy because of the pre-Tridentine training of *ex opere operato* we mentioned earlier. Yet on the other hand, most of us are totally unimpressed by the borderline histrionics of some prayer leaders who seem to be undergoing a total ecstatic rapture as they make their prayer, especially the ones who can be seen on late-night TV in some areas of the US.

To be fair, the existence of both extremes can (at least partly) be laid at the feet of cultural traditions which radically impact our style of prayer and the expectations held by our respective communities. After all, prayer, an ancient human activity of communication, is impacted by the very same things that impact other communications, including local culture. I remember my first week as a hospice chaplain in the East Bay (California) cities of Oakland, Richmond, and others, and going with one of the social workers to visit a female patient who was a member of a

Black Baptist church and who had a group of ladies from the church visiting when we arrived. The visit was wonderful, but it was like nothing I'd ever experienced in my white, English, Catholic upbringing. As the visit came to a close, the social worker asked the patient if she wanted me to say a prayer with her. The patient looked at me and asked, "How long you been a chaplain?" I replied it was my first week, to which she responded, "Oh heck, I think we better pray for you!" And they did, with the laying on of hands and many "hmmm-mmms" and "thank you Jesus" along the way. I have to say, I felt prayed for in a way I've experienced very few times before or since in my life. Why? They had a complete integration of their intent, their words, and their body and breath in that time and place. As a colleague remarked later as I told the story, "Oh yeah, even God wouldn't dare not show up in that situation." I totally agree!

Why did the experience feel so powerful to me? (And I realize I'm using the word "feel," so this is about my experience, not to what extent the Divine was impressed or impacted by it.) It felt authentic. These women didn't know me, but they gifted me with their kindness, their humor, and their love. In all the visits I made after that to this East Bay community, I had their example as a guide and a standard. My job was to be, for a few moments, a voice for the kindness, humor, healing power, and love of God, and not to be only about known formulas or prescribed prayers. For those who were used to, and expected, a prayer from a book, they were available too. In either case, what was most important was that I had to learn to turn up in person, because that's what the situation demanded. I admit my first "we just thank you, Jesus . . ." probably didn't sound very convinced or convincing, but it got better! (This is the reality of the "10,000 hours of practice" mentioned earlier.) I learned to find my honest self in the words they needed, rather than only in the words I was used to, and I realized this is what an actor does when we use someone else's words to speak in a play. In the same way, a chaplain or presider is called to speak in the words that the recipient can understand.

THE PRACTICE OF LEARNING YOUR LINES

As someone who has had to "learn my lines" over the decades, I've come to realize that (a) I can assimilate lines quicker in the morning, especially over breakfast, than later in the day and (b) I remember the lines better when I understand the actions and feelings that go with them. While many actors are great at learning all their lines before the first rehearsal, I was always grateful if that wasn't required. When the day would come during the rehearsal period when we had to put the scripts down, even if I was only holding mine as a sort-of security blanket at that point, I always found that I forgot many of them the next time through. The rehearsal process of moving from first read to performance is an amazing period (usually four to six weeks, three to five times a week) of *working* to own the lines, find the character, and establish on-stage relationships.

Like the experience with prayer, the process is always a journey into authenticity, into self- and character-discovery. And it's the work of all our professions.

When a presider is leading a service with a community, often in a church space, the challenges are similar yet also different. As we prepare to use any prescribed prayers from a church book, we're invited to spend time with them and experience them firsthand. Just as an actor, even if taking part in a table-read or a staged reading, would never dream of turning up without first going over the script, maybe even with a pencil for marking observations, no presider should dream of leading a scripted prayer in a community without making it their own first. An impromptu or spontaneous prayer obviously comes out of the person and the moment. But when we're required to give that level of connection and commitment to the words of another, we must make them our own first if we're going to be authentic.

This brings us to the question of "how does one speak to God?" An actor usually speaks to another person on stage, but even so, their effort is pointless if the audience can't hear or understand what's been said. In a similar way, while a presider might be addressing the Almighty on the community's behalf, it's essential that the congregation can both hear and understand what's being said. We're speaking on their behalf, and usually also inviting their "amen" in affirmation of what's been said. This may seem obvious, but that doesn't mean affirmation always happens.

THE MECHANICS OF PUBLIC SPEAKING

In terms of the mechanics of public speaking, when I work with community theater companies and college student productions, I suggest they think of their voice as if it were coming out of a loudspeaker, the output for which is controlled by four knobs or dials which represented volume, pitch, articulation, and intention.

Issues around volume are obvious, and includes projection. Volume and projection are most significantly affected by breath: the more you have to use, the louder you can be and the further the sound can carry. If you are not breathing properly you will not have the breath required for the job. One can put all the intention in the world into a sentence, but if no one can hear it, it's for nought! For those who have the benefit (or challenge) of microphones, testing them regularly is worthwhile. Spaces good for music are frequently poor for the spoken word. Getting professional help is highly recommended for any sound system, which almost everyone seems to be using these days. Every diocese or convention should, I suggest, have a network of specialists available to help with this. Any diocese or convention that spends time, energy, and money training their community leaders as communicators but fails to provide them with the technological support to do the job is only doing half the job. Projection is largely about placement of the voice in the resonating cavities between the chest and face. If you wish to improve yours, take classical singing lessons.

Pitch is a harder issue and relates to the vocal range of the speaker. As an exercise I ask students to listen to radio announcers, especially ones at the BBC, who are particularly good at using a wide range of pitch as they make announcements or read the news. Similarly, most of us are familiar with singers vocalizing from one end of their range to the other and back again, ensuring that their tessitura (the technical term for "range") is sufficient for a particular song or role; but one rarely hears anyone else, apart from professional actors, developing that potential in their voices. Without flexibility in pitch, one ends up using a very narrow range of notes; and yes, speakers use notes just as much as singers. We all know what a monotonous voice sounds like. "Mono-tone-ous" literally meaning "using one note." Need more be said? The average mature human voice has a range of at least one octave (that's 12 notes on the piano) and frequently nearly two. If you have three or more octaves, you're in a league with the likes of Beyoncé, Tina Turner, and Michael Jackson, along with professional classical vocalists.

For speakers, a lack of willingness to use your vocal range can be a product of cultural conditioning as much as anything. Some cultures and accents tend towards the monotone and use a somewhat limited range of notes when speaking. Using anything like your available vocal range in such social environments might lead one to being ridiculed and mocked. To "find one's voice" after growing up in such a culture can be a journey of its own. Alternatively for some cultures (including some in the American South and the people of Wales in the UK), "singsong" is often used to describe their voices, and they naturally use much more of their available range than natives from other places. We rarely need anything like Beyoncé, Tina, or Michael's range, but more than two or three notes is absolutely required from anyone in the public arena.

Also likely to open one to ridicule is point three, learning how to articulate your words. Frequently regarded as "being aloof" or a snob, articulating clearly is, in much of today's society, regarded as fake or worse. One can have great volume and variety of pitch, but if the words are not discernible then, again, what's the point? Articulation is hard if you came from a culture where final consonants are not sounded and where whole words are reduced to partial words. If one then adds onto that a noticeable regional accent, verbal communication with anyone other than your neighbors becomes significantly more difficult. Please don't take this as meaning I don't like regional accents; I truly do. However, just like on the stage, in church one must learn how to balance all the "knobs" mentioned above so that the job is done, and people, especially visitors and strangers, can hear and understand you.

Some will suggest that the presider and preacher should learn to sound like the people whom they serve, which is also an important parameter to engage, to some extent. After the first homily I gave in America, several parishioners said, "We love your accent! We can't understand a word you're saying, but we love your accent!" The same can be true for presiders and preachers moving around just their own country, let alone an adopted one. The balancing act we each have to learn is how to be understood while at the same time not surrendering our own voice. Currently my voice is somewhere in the mid-Atlantic; I sound English or Australian to an American, but American to a Brit. I continually have to work to be understood on either side of the "pond," meaning that paying attention to my pace (not talking too quickly) and articulation are always appropriate and required.

All these elements work together to support the fourth dial, expressing the meaning or intention of the script. As we mentioned earlier, words, phrases, and sentences can mean more than one thing, and we can change the meaning depending on the intentionality and intonation we bring to our voice, as well as our facial and other features. If expressing intention is the prime purpose of what we are about in our work (hopefully to find numerous ways to say, "God loves you"), then we must use all the skills at our disposal to help make that happen.

Spoken words do real work. They can heal, they can wound, and they can inspire or put down. Consequentially, having a very clear idea of what work we're trying to do with the words we speak is essential.

CHOOSING THE SCRIPT

As most reading this book will already know, Christian prayers come in four basic varieties, known by the acronym ACTS, which stands for Adoration, Contrition, Thanksgiving, and Supplication. Prayers said by most of us in these four categories are usually simple, direct, and heartfelt. They come spontaneously, not from a script (unless it's the Lord's Prayer), and they're to the point, sometimes consisting of just the single word "Help!" They're motivated by the moment. Most of the time we follow Jesus' instructions and pray them in the privacy of our own rooms, behind closed doors (Mt. 6:6), or silently in a church or other special place, such as a hospital bedside.

When one is asked to pray in public (a grace before a meal or meeting, an invocation at a school graduation, the blessing of a team), a second dimension opens—the cultural, theological, and linguistic expectations and judgment of those listening and for whom we are speaking. Ask an Irish Catholic priest in Chicago, a Southern Baptist minister in rural Louisiana, and an Episcopal pastor in California to pray on the same subject, (such as a meal blessing, or before a sports game), and you'll hear three very different prayers. The intent might be exactly the same, but they'll be expressed very differently. The delightful and rich cultural, theological, and linguistic idioms of the three individuals and their respective backgrounds and cultural contexts will color their words. These occasions are also very educational (even if that isn't their intention) as they model for those listening how they might pray too.

When one belongs to a church which provides texts for prayers, and especially for liturgical prayers, then we generally lose any specific cultural and linguistic quality and are left with the theological. We also tend to find that a very intentional theologically-focused educational dimension exists to these prayers too. Read these prayers and you'll find that we rehearse over and over the story of our salvation, or what the theologians call the *anamnesis* or remembering. However, the context is as if we were reminding God of what God has done, not reminding ourselves. An excellent example of this is the opening section of Eucharistic Prayer IV of the Roman Church. It starts well enough ("We give you praise, Father most holy, for you are great . . .") but then the writers distance themselves from the community and the present moment:

> *We give you praise, Father most holy, for you are great, and you have fashioned all your works in wisdom and in love. You formed man in your own image and entrusted the whole world to his care, so that in serving you alone, the Creator, he might have dominion over all creatures.*
>
> *And when through disobedience he had lost your friendship, you did not abandon him to the domain of death. For you came in mercy to the aid of all, so that those who seek might find you. Time and again you offered them covenants and through the prophets taught them to look forward to salvation.*

Within the Christian faith tradition, all this is true (apart from the gendered language,) and fundamental. Our repetition of the story is crucially important. *Anamnesis* is, after all, the opposite to *amnesia*, another Greek word, and reminds us that the stories we fail to repeat, even though they ground us in our being, will cause us to forget who we truly are. The way the prayer is crafted, however, especially the use of a distancing "him" rather than a personalizing "us," as well as the past tense, creates distance and separation. Read the prayer again with these simple changes to continue the "we" theme of the opening, but not changing any of the theology (emphasis mine):

> *We give you praise, Father most holy, for you are great, and you have fashioned all your works in wisdom and in love. **We thank you for forming us** in your own image and **entrusting** the whole world to **our** care, so that in serving you alone, the Creator, **we** might have dominion* (although I would rather say "stewardship" or "responsibility") *over all creatures.*
>
> *And when through disobedience **we lose** your friendship, you **do not abandon us** to the domain of death. For you **come** in mercy to the aid of all, so that those who seek might find you. Time and again you offered **us** covenants and through the prophets taught **us** to look forward to salvation.*

With these words the presider is now truly speaking for the congregation, and they can hear themselves mirrored in the words. "We" are now praying. The former wording is what's known in a theatrical script as "exposition" (filling in the background and useful facts) and is generally regarded as something that should be kept to a minimum. The latter version creates a dialogue in the present moment which connects the past with the future. It also encourages the congregation to say an internal "yes" to this ongoing relationship. Howe's trinity is more clearly manifested: With the words more carefully crafted (or communicated), a relationship is more easily created, and change becomes a more real possibility.

From the perspective, therefore, of the script, we need to own up to the fact that most prayers written by official church bodies will be theologically "correct" (if one believes in substitutional atonement theology) but often lack the human touch. Similarly, using the original script and ignoring a specific cultural or linguistic context, the presider has to work harder to engage the emotions, feelings, imagination, or hearts of the people because the prayer, written about "him" and set in the past, is not grounded in these qualities in the present moment.

I bring this up to point out the challenge for the presider of repeatedly proclaiming these or similar words as the mouthpiece of the congregation in a world which is no longer a sixteenth- or seventeenth-century model. Our contemporary reality needs a script which is "fit for service" as well as still fits with the Tradition. Such a script is not difficult, but composing it is work.

For playgoers, transformation is rarely affected by an individual actor or moment but by the experience of the whole play, for the parts are not divisible in their efficacy. Out of its context, an amazing moment rarely works. Some parts might stand out and help us have that "ah-ha" experience, but they're nothing without their context. Similarly in church, any action towards change is not affected by the priest or others alone, but by the Holy Spirit, which is symbolically carried on the breath of the words we all speak and sing.

The invitation revealed is therefore: Are we working hard enough? Are we developing our communication skills keenly enough to be vehicles for that potential transformation which Jesus and the Good News offers, even if transformation is not the primary reason the people come? The Holy Spirit is experienced at working through humans to reach other humans but, as the well-worn phrase goes, "You gotta give me something to work with!" And the more we can give the Spirit to work with, especially our deep intentionality and humble honesty in our enfleshed speaking and proclaiming, the more the Spirit can work with it.

If we were looking for a community discussion topic, we may ask how well all the hundreds of millions of words we've spoken in church have worked. If one is looking to judge the efficacy of all that communication by viewing the actions of the Christians who heard them, then clearly we have, in almost every age, a very wide range of results, everything from shining and almost-universally recognized saints (as well as many hidden ones) to total creeps and hideous monsters, both exposed and unnoticed, with most of us somewhere in the middle. If Jesus' suggestion that "by their fruits shall you know them" (Mt 7:15–20) is true, what do we know about our services when we look at Christians in today's world?

THE PREACHER AS WORDSMITH AND ORATOR

The role of the preacher is unique in this regard. They get to be their own monologue writer and presenter (though, like their late-night counterparts, this monologue is actually a dialogue between them and the audience). While late-night TV hosts have an entire writing staff to help them prepare, the average preacher has just themself to rely on, yet must create a significant piece of thinking and then communicate it every time they stand in front of their community. Both content and delivery need to be effective. And, given that most have the same audience members every week, unlike a stand-up comedian they can't re-use their work as they travel through each new town they visit. The pressure and the level of expectation is huge. If one is called to this role without the requisite gifts and charisms, fulfilling the calling is effectively impossible.

Some preachers use a script, others work from notes, while yet others "freestyle" from start to finish. One of the hardest aspects of preaching without preparing a script is that the ending isn't necessarily arrived at effectively and with an appropriate sense of resolution. Not preparing a script can be like the effect of ending a piece of music by forgetting to play the last few bars. One reason is that preachers are storytellers, and storytellers have to know the ending before they can plot the path from the start. Any catharsis comes from the resolution of the ideas and subplots that have been woven throughout the piece, so that the ending gets its appropriate "punch" and energy. Significant skill is needed to do that off-the-cuff without a clear plan. Or, to put it another way, just because you are working without a script doesn't mean you should be working without preparation.

Working without a script is similar to taking a journey. One knows where one is starting, but myriad options are available for where, when, and how one ends. One cannot plot the path until that decision is made. One can, of course, wander aimlessly, which can be very fruitful when one is beginning work on a sermon, letting the mind wander and seeing what comes up, rather like an enjoyable Sunday afternoon trip in the car. Such meandering is not, however, recommended as a model for any form of preaching if you expect anyone to return the following week.

Knowing how to end a piece is a major part of the craft of being an artist, whether it's a piece of music, a poem, a painting, a play, piece of sculpture, or a sermon. It is well known, for example, that J.K. Rowling wrote the last chapter of the final "Harry Potter" book before writing Book 1. Such knowledge is also true for the evangelists who penned the gospels. They could only write their version of the Jesus story because they had experienced, (most likely at second hand), the earthly ending. They chose to start at three rather different places. Both Luke and Matthew shared the birth story as their starting point, though they approached even that differently; but they, along with Mark and John, all journey towards Jerusalem and death, and of course resurrection. The ending is actually much more important than the beginning, which can be almost anywhere. In most cases when one is preaching one can (and one might even say should) choose your beginning to make the journey clearer for the listener. On the other hand, an unexpected starting point might be better at grabbing the listener's attention.

I'm always reminded of the old Irish story of a lost driver stopping in a small rural village and asking for directions to Dublin, to which a local replies, "Ah, to be sure, if I was going there, I wouldn't start from here at all!"

All of this is easier to do if one is preparing a script, even if one doesn't use it on the day. Few of us are talented enough to neatly tie off all the ends on the spot, even as we're creating a sermon in front of a congregation. That doesn't mean of course that one always gets to write one's homily, and that we should never speak unless we've fully prepared. Both eventualities happen many times in a preacher's life, and even have some wonderful outcomes. However, as a rule, I don't encourage people to rely on "in the moment talent" if they're speaking in front of the same crowd week after week. Even Shakespeare, Chekhov and Jerry Seinfeld only use a limited number of themes.

KNOWING AND DELIVERING YOUR LINES

While many fine books are available to help preachers, COVID has given us a burst of new, actual examples on the internet. Just as actors watch other actors to help analyze and absorb the talent, so too can ministers. In my experience, few preachers have more than one basic style, one main message, and one well-used structure for delivery. That was probably the main example on which they have been fed since childhood. Preachers who are worth traveling for and listening to are few and far between. I would suggest that this isn't due to a total lack of talent or desire to communicate effectively but rather habit combined with a lack of training and development.

I once taught a preaching class and invited each person to bring one homily message or theme (based on a passage of scripture) about which they felt enthusiastic and excited. I then asked them to find three distinct ways to preach that message. Examples we discussed included:

- As a telephone conversation with God, where only the human side is heard
- As a poem
- As a contemporary fairytale
- As the closing argument in a court trial
- As the reminiscences of a person thinking back on their life
- As a monologue (or dialogue if working with a partner) by one of the people in the chosen biblical story, telling a friend sometime later what happened and how it affected them
- As a TV reporter describing interviewing the people involved with the story and what they saw and heard, and the aftermath

(For a couple of examples of these approaches, see the Appendix.)

The purpose was to encourage the preachers not just to ask themselves what needed to be said but *how* to say it. We've all heard the adage that "the medium is the message," so the invitation was to explore how flexible and attentive they were to the various mediums available in the spoken word. The books of the Jewish scriptures give us numerous examples of this, so the concept is not un-biblical.

If one is going to call oneself a preacher, or accept the calling as an archetype and title, then one must accept the responsibility to learn as much as possible about how to communicate the message, not just discover what the message is. The good news is that you probably have very few restrictions except your own skill and creativity, and the further good news is that classes exist to help.

AND IF YOU FORGET YOUR LINES?

We all get our lines wrong and sometimes we forget them. What matters most is that we remain honest, authentic (to ourselves and/or the character), and humble in the moment, and then move forward.

Whether I am performer, presider, or preacher, I am always, first and foremost, human. I may need to apologize. I may need to laugh at myself. Ad libbing a transitional comment may be appropriate or returning to simply restate correctly what I said incorrectly. And sometimes, if the misstep is minor, I just let it go and move on. Don't get lost in the error, but neither be defensive nor deny it. Breathe. Maybe smile and carry on.

Our rituals, when they're successful, celebrate humanity infused with the Divine. And the Divine has been working with, and doing improv with, mere humans for quite a while, so God will cope, whatever happens!

BEWARE ATTEMPTING THE PERFECT LITURGY!

One Easter Triduum I attended a Catholic university chapel, knowing that their worship team was very committed to creating beautiful, thoughtful worship. I had attended some of their Lenten services and they were appropriate and very well organized. And indeed, that Holy Thursday service, especially the washing the feet, was executed with military precision. The Easter vigil service was very beautiful, well organized, and flowed like a well-oiled machine, from darkness, to fire, to water, to light and thanksgiving. All great, except it was totally soulless, with no sense of joy or surprise. How can you sing so many "Alleluias" without smiling? It totally lacked humanity. The phrase used earlier of "all production, no content" felt true.

All liturgy and worship is an action of the people. It *has* to be fully human!

Give me a moment or two of "oops!" with an appropriate grimace or laugh and "sorry!" over a service where no space has been left to be real. The Divine Real Presence is guaranteed by Jesus, "wherever two or three are gathered . . ." However, it is the real presence of human beings which makes the gathering an act of worship.

The reason we fully prepare our lines, get our costumes looking right, don't distract with unnecessary actions or movements and the like is not to make the worship "perfect." It is to help us as ministers and people relax, able to trust the structure, like the scaffolding around a building, that frees us to be our fullest human selves in the moment.

I remember a fitness coach once saying that one of the reasons we should get fit is not just for the benefits of the workouts, but that our recovery time improves. If I must exert myself but it takes me three days to recover, then I am not fit. If I can return to a sense of "center" in just three minutes, then I am more fit, and able to continue. When an "unplanned human moment" happens in worship, can we respond appropriately, and then recover, return to center, and continue? Or are we and the people distracted for the rest of our time together? Experienced performers, presiders and preachers are people who can recover when something "unplanned" happens and return to center, with the flow not broken.

I was once officiating a wedding in a vineyard, (very biblical I thought!) and as the groom was giving the bride her ring and repeating after me "Julie, take this ring," he dropped it. He looked at me in horror. I simply smiled, glance down at the ring, as if to say, "pick it up" and continued by saying, "blessed by the earth," which he repeated, as he did the rest of the text. I added the same phrase in the bride's words, even though she didn't drop anything. (I suspect she nearly did, just to match. That would have been delightful!)

As many religions teach, only the Divine is perfect. Our job is to be human. The reason we prepare is not to be perfect, but to be relaxed and confident so we can be really present and serve, with trust in that moment of grace, whatever happens.

QUESTIONS FOR REFLECTION

1. When and where do you go to hear great sermons and homilies? What do you learn from them in terms of both content and delivery?
2. Have you ever worked with a voice coach to see what potential you have within your own vocal instrument? How do you prepare your voice, along with your body and breath, for every liturgy?
3. Do you feel inhibited by the culture and norms of your community? Are you afraid of being your best, most gifted self in your ministry?

4. Would you consider learning your regular prayers by heart and proclaiming them from that place? Would you risk taking the time to simply "say" the words just as you mean them, not as is usually done in your community? (One thinks of the Lord's Prayer, the creeds, the confession., etc.)

10

Dress Rehearsal and Opening Night, and the Joy and Monotony of a Long Run

Approach every script and presentation as if the ink is still wet!

I REMEMBER A PRODUCTION of *La Cage aux Folles* in Richmond, west of London in the UK. They had rented the sets (and costumes) from the original London West End production, and they were amazing. However, they had been two days late arriving, and were so large that the company never had a full test run before opening night. And, remembering the term from earlier, the "rake" (slope) on that particular stage is quite severe.

The consequence was that the door in the first set started opening by itself because of gravity, which was funny, but when we in the audience heard a loud "oops!" from backstage, and saw the whole back wall slowly start slipping towards us, it was a little scary, especially for those at the front. Four stagehands had to come on and hold the large back piece in place until the end of the scene. Things evolved (or rather devolved) from there! Luckily the cast were truly excellent, and the audience took the mishaps all in their collective stride. (Friends and family tend to come to opening nights, so that probably helped.)

We reached the last scene, and George, the narrator character, was setting up the finale with the audience when he got to his last line and began, "And so, ladies and gentlemen . . ." when a voice from offstage shouted, "We're not ready!" The actor looked horrified, but luckily the audience clapped and cheered. George then spent ten minutes ad-libbing with the audience until the same voice shouted "Okay!" At this point the embarrassing chaos was all part of the show! George finished his original lines and then added, "And yes, someone back there will die tonight!" We all cheered!

Suffice to say that was a memorable opening night, even over thirty years later. These structural missteps were a great shame because, as I said, the performances and everything else were excellent. The cast (including those backstage) did a magnificent job of "staying calm and carrying on" as the old wartime motto recommends. But I don't think they were happy, and I suspect an extra "run-through" was called for at 10am the next morning to sort it all out. Unfortunately, what was meant to be a glorious opening night (it was a full house), was really a very challenging final dress rehearsal. Such things happen.

Theater dress rehearsals are almost always required; or, if one is in a traveling show at a new venue, if not a full rehearsal, then at least a walk-through of all entrances and exits,. No one in their right mind would normally go on without one. Even weddings have them these days, giving all the bridesmaids and groomsmen a chance to learn where to stand, and what to do (smile) and not do (put your hands in your pockets) on the big day.

Great rituals are also always rehearsed, or at least one hopes so. We hear that a royal funeral in England is practiced at least once a year, and sometimes more often if a significant change of important personnel happens, or the event is becoming more likely. Similarly, the 2023 coronation of King Charles III had to be rehearsed both with and without the main characters on more than one occasion. The Olympic opening ceremony in Paris was rehearsed in the middle of night as it was the only time the streets and River Seine were clear. The truth is, if a thing is worth doing well, it's worth rehearsing.

In most churches the choir rehearses weekly, and major events for the acolytes and other altar servers are rehearsed each time they come around. Clergy and even lay leaders are less consistent about rehearsing; mainly, of course, because they're doing basically the same thing every week in the same venue, so they rarely feel they need it unless a special change or event is happening, like the diocesan bishop is visiting. However, that doesn't mean the clergy won't need feedback or, to use another theater term, production notes when a long run has allowed small unintended changes or mistakes to become habits.

Over time, be it a long theater run or the repetitiveness of fifty-two Sundays a year, habits can creep in with consequences that might not be intended. Feedback is needed to see if this helps or hinders the flow of the script. For example, unless you're suffering from a condition that makes drinking water in the middle of a service essential to doing your job, please don't do it. It's saying to the congregation, "I'm not actually paying attention to this part, so you don't have to either if you don't want to." The distraction is disrespectful and, I feel, rude. This is also the message when a presider starts giving instructions to a server to do something during a reading or song, or starts flicking through a service book to find their next lines. The message is, "This is all about me; the rest of them aren't essential."

The other common distraction (and that's why these issues are important—they distract from the quality and flow of the ritual) is when a presider isn't comfortable in their clothes or vestments, or the microphone has been attached at the wrong point. I remember one service where the presider was using an "over the ear" microphone. These can be a very good choice, as they don't catch on your clothes or vestments, and they remain the same distance from your mouth even when you turn your head. However, this presider also wanted to play his guitar, and so every time he put the guitar strap over his head, he hit the mic. It was a simple solution to suggest he wear the earpiece over the other ear (which wasn't affected by the strap), but no one had ever suggested it before because, well, he's the pastor!

Microphones are their own topic, both on stage and in the sanctuary. When attached to clothes they can be balanced for sound when one speaks facing forward, but will be potentially out of alignment when one turns one's head to the left or right, causing the volume to fluctuate. The same is true for microphones on a stand, as at a lectern or pulpit. Lectors, cantors, announcers, preachers, and presiders all need to learn to speak into or across the head of microphone. This is why theater folk place them next to an ear, or in the hair of the actor, with a lead going down their back to the power pack.

Vestments should be the right size, worn correctly, clean and (if necessary) pressed, or please don't bother. You won't see a reputable theater company allow a person to be on stage in anything more or less than what's appropriate for telling you who and what the character is. As we've said earlier, everything communicates, both individually and as a collection. One can't stop people receiving the communication of whatever you do and say, and how you act in the ritual space. Ritual clothing has a specific function, and although such clothing is not actually essential in Christian ritual (except maybe the stole for some), it's there to help create the space where the sacred and sacrament can happen in the Tradition of the community.

Another tradition in the theater which churches might learn from is about jewelry, even "ordinary" stuff like watches and wedding rings. In the theater the rule is to ask the question, "What jewelry would the character wear?" If the answer is "nothing," that means putting a flesh-colored bandage over a wedding ring so that it "disappears." (Some actors are comfortable taking off a wedding ring, others aren't, so we work with that.) For presiders, my rule is that a simple wedding ring is acceptable and, if necessary, simple stud earrings if you have pierced ears, but nothing else—no watch, necklaces, broaches, cufflinks, or other displays of wealth or status. Non-ritual jewelry is designed and worn to be noticed, and when you're leading a ritual they're a distraction to the congregation, as they're about you and not about the job, the work, or the function. For lectors and preachers who aren't wearing ritual clothing, tasteful jewelry that doesn't distract should be fine. But please remember to turn off your phone or watch! And if your watch lights up even in "silent mode" put it in your pocket or bag.

In the theater inviting professional colleagues to attend dress rehearsals to give last-minute feedback and maybe notice things which the production's team (director, assistant, stage manager, etc.) have missed isn't uncommon. I'm always very grateful to such colleagues over the years, as they often notice things to which I had been blind. (The old adage "familiarity breeds contempt" comes to mind.)

You've probably also heard about "out of town try-outs" for new productions. This is where a show that's headed for a major venue, maybe on New York's Broadway or London's West End, starts at a smaller venue to gauge audience reaction and build familiarity and comfort for the actors as well as test the script. These tryouts are an opportunity for the writer and/or composer to fine-tune the script and score. Just as we heard earlier about becoming a minister, it can take time in front of an audience for an actor to "become one" with a character. One can rehearse for weeks, but until you take that performance in front of an audience, you'll never truly know if it works or what it needs if it doesn't.

I well remember the first time I presided at a eucharist. I had preached before and led several other services, but that first mass with a congregation was a revelation. Rather like my experience years later with the Black Baptist women of Richmond around a patient's bed, the experience might have been better if that congregation had just prayed for me! But I got through it and did my best, which is all any of us can do. Years later I often still have the same fears and concerns. I've come to a better understanding of my relationship to the One who is truly the Priest and the One whose action is transforming the moment through the humans gathered around the altar table. I'm a part of a team, and I've learned to try to trust my colleagues, human and Divine, more completely. But I still get nervous every time.

THE CALL—NO, NOT THAT ONE!

Most folks will be familiar with a person saying they feel they have a "call" to ministry. However, in the theater we get an actual call thirty or sixty minutes before every show, and then usually at the fifteen-minute mark (which is twenty minutes before the curtain goes up) and five minutes (ten minutes before curtain). And yes, as you'll notice, we assume everyone and everything will be ready five minutes before the advertised start time. Also, when the stage manager (SM) announces, for example, "Ladies and gentlemen, this is your fifteen-minute call, fifteen minutes please, everyone," everyone replies, "Thank you, fifteen." It's all very civilized!

Actors are usually initially called one hour before show time, unless you've been given a special dispensation by the SM; for example, if you aren't in the first half of the show. The SM is the person in absolute charge once the final dress rehearsal is finished. At least one hour before show time, you arrive in the dressing room area and sign in. Anyone not signed in when the SM checks the list is *late!* This is regarded as unprofessional and rude, and a serious apology is expected to everyone. A complex set or costume change might also be rehearsed every night before the show. Fight scenes are *required* to be rehearsed every night, so some folks might be called even earlier. Complex hair and makeup requirements can also necessitate earlier calls. If characters/dancers are required to do lifts in the production, those too will normally be rehearsed every night before the thirty-minute call.

Even if the show is a one-person show with normal street clothes and no special makeup, being there and preparing at least thirty-five minutes before show time is normal. And even if that one performer is their own director, the SM is still in charge. I don't know many clergy who maintain such a serious and rigorous commitment to their ritual schedule and are also willing to surrender their "primacy" offstage so easily. On the other hand, of course, many clergy are their own SMs, so we can see where the problem lies.

Sometime between the thirty- and fifteen-minute calls, the SM will announce that the stage must be cleared. Until that call, actors are welcome to move around the set, do warm-ups, practice difficult sections, stretch, and generally "feel at home" in the space. Crew can adjust lights, set pieces, add props and the like. However, the audience is not there. Once the "clear the stage, please" announcement has been given, the SM will then inform the front-of-house manager (FHM) that "the house may be opened" and the audience can be admitted. As you can probably imagine, the traditional proscenium arch from which hangs the front curtain (or the modern equivalent if no curtain exists) is the dividing line between the areas of responsibility of the SM and the FHM.

In larger spaces, the SM and FHM each might also have their own staff. For example, the SM will often have an assistant as well as stagehands for moving sets during the show, technical staff (in the tech booth) to control lights and sound, along with (depending on the show) dressers, makeup artists, and others. The FHM will have box office staff, ushers, maybe a coatroom check person, loop-system attendant (for the hard of hearing) and then bar and refreshment staff for before the show and during any intermission. If an audience member has a problem or question, it's directed to the FHM.

When start time nears, the SM will ask the FHM if everything is ready on their side of the curtain. Once the FHM is confident that everyone is settled and in good order, they will tell the SM they can take over, who will then give the cue for the house lights to be dimmed and the show to begin. The handover process is repeated in miniature at any intermission.

This procedure happens every night, up to eight shows a week, for the entire run, whether the show is big and performed by professionals or small and performed by a local community theater company, a local high school or a large regional college or university. Yes, scale differs, of course, but the tradition, the structure, the rituals are all the same. And they're sacred to those who have been initiated into this international theater community. This structure is what builds a sense of family, of mutual responsibility, of care for the final production and each other, as well as communicating with the audience. Act like you're better than your theater family and don't need them, and you won't survive long in the profession. Without individual humility and care for the team, the process all falls apart. If you want to experience a world where people say "thank you" to each other a lot, from directors to janitors, join a theater community.

Can you say that about your local church community? I sincerely hope so. Are all the candles lit, ritual items in the correct place, and all "cast" members dressed and either greeting congregants at the door or in their place, ready to begin thirty or even fifteen minutes before the beginning of the service? Whether in a theater or a church, this level of hospitality is the way we show respect for the covenant between the cast and crew or ministers and the people. A theatre company would not dream of leaving set pieces or props from a previous production around for a new show but, for example, I've been in churches where it's not clear which season we are in.

The call to Christian ministry is, according to our twenty-first century understanding of theology, a facet of the priesthood of the whole people of God with the risen Christ as its head as the one high priest. Ordained priesthood, and all other ministries, only exist because the whole community is the living body of Christ and therefore priest, prophet, and sovereign over death in this world through the person and the life, as well as the death and resurrection of Jesus. Divas and divos are no more appropriate or welcome in liturgy as they are on stage. They do, of course, happen in both worlds, but without true humility such individuals will ultimately fail to grow as human beings, and will be remembered not for their gifts but their failings.

IN IT FOR THE LONG RUN

Doing anything the same way every day, whether presiding at liturgy, acting in or helping to run a show, or any other occupation, can easily tend to the monotonous. Of course, people who like their lives to be fixed and scheduled and for whom consistency is a true gift are among us. However, on a continuum from "always the same" to "never the same," I hope "some diversity is the spice of life" is nearer to the truth of the majority.

For both ministers and actors, if they're in a job that has the security of a long run, they'll need to find that which makes each occasion new if they're to avoid performing by rote or being accused of "phoning it in" without the necessary energy. That's not to say that every occasion needs to have the energy of an Easter Vigil or Broadway opening night. That would be exhausting. I remember a professional dancer confiding after a performance in which they'd received rave reviews that they'd been very preoccupied with plans for a dinner the next evening, and their mind wasn't really on the task at hand at all, but were just in muscle memory mode. I also remember a vocal professor explaining to a class of classical singers that, as their careers developed, they would need to find the spiritual focus that enabled them to perform their tenth *Messiah* or Bach B Minor Mass of the season with sufficient commitment so as to carry the message of the music, not just the notes, whether the message was their own spiritual truth or not. "That is, after all," he said, "what you are being paid to do."

This excerpt from an article in *The Guardian* newspaper is pertinent:

> *Dustin Hoffman has long been known as one of method acting's most earnest exponents. A showbiz story involves his collaboration with Laurence Olivier on the 1976 film* Marathon Man. *Upon being asked by his co-star how a previous scene had gone, one in which Hoffman's character had supposedly stayed up for three days, Hoffman admitted that he too had not slept for 72 hours to achieve emotional verisimilitude. "My dear boy," replied Olivier smoothly, "why don't you just try acting?" (Hoffman subsequently attributed his insomnia to excessive partying rather than artistry.)*[1]

Some preparatory actions might be appropriate for the medium of film, but over the nightly run of a stage show one might have numerous emotions, and one can't take a twenty-minute break in between each scene to "refocus" one's energy. Part of the skill and training needed is the ability to bring up the appropriate words and emotion at the appropriate time. We are, therefore, correct to think of muscle memory mode as a useful and even necessary ability for performers. Each person must find a balance between muscle memory and spontaneous authenticity to enable them to respond to any slight shift in a colleague's performance or the audience's attention in order to keep the focus and energy moving in the necessary

---

1. Michael Simkins, *The Guardian*, March 2016.

direction. What's most important is that the audience or congregation cannot see the difference and the focus all stays "in the moment."

I remember doing a short run of the play *Not About Heroes* by Stephen MacDonald, a "based on real facts" two-hander about World War One poets Siegfried Sassoon and Wilfred Owens, who met at a hospital in Scotland for war-wounded soldiers. As Sassoon, every night I had to grow to care about, even love (platonically) this young yet brilliant upstart (Owens), only to be completely devastated by his death in battle one week before the end of hostilities. The purpose of the rehearsal time was to find the necessary and right emotions and muscle memory, which could then be relied on during the run, and not have only raw emotion in my toolbox. That I should cry on stage was unimportant (I didn't in production, though I did copiously in some rehearsals) but that the audience might be brought to tears. I was there to engender emotion in the audience, not in myself. Having an emotional "muscle memory" really helped. I was still greatly moved each night, but I wasn't a wreck!

As a presider and preacher, we get to tell a story of great love and generosity and, every time, also suffering and death too. Up to seventy years ago the tradition may have been to stay with the suffering and death longer, and focus one's energy on making sure each member of the congregation felt personally responsible for it, even though it happened almost two thousand years ago. Today we start, (I hope!) with Jesus' life and end with the resurrection, for only with the balance of Good News amid the rest is it sustainable to endure. As we've mentioned, many if not most theologians today no longer focus on substitutionary atonement theology as the primary way of understanding the Jesus story. The lens through which we understand the facts, with modern scripture and historical study, like the re-visioning of a production to stage a script and therefore create a play, has brought new themes and ways of understanding to light.

If an actor is exploring their relationships with the others on stage as well as with themselves, so a preacher or presider is fundamentally exploring their relationship with those Divine actors we mentioned earlier (Creator, Savior, Inspirer), along with the community they're leading. In the moment of a live production or a liturgy, these relationships can shift. Just as an actor explores the onstage relationships in connection to their own character during the rehearsal period, then continues to develop them during the run of the show, so a preacher and presider comes to know themself in relation to their God and the people of God they're serving in a similar way, by practice.

As with most relationships in our life, dull days, quiet days, and days of immense celebration happen, along with everything in between. Similarly, things will change depending on the energy and authenticity we bring to those days together, as well as outside events. All our established relationships have a base line which is how we know one another and greet one another, based on our past connections. We don't start from scratch each time we meet. In the same way, a preacher or presider is building a relationship and base line with the congregation they serve over time. The more honest and authentic that relationship is, and the more both parties can be present to the relationship, the more it can be trusted to weather the ups and downs of their communal life.

In this way a sustainable long run, whether in a personal relationship, as an actor on stage in a show, or as a leading member of a faith community, can best be created by authentic self-presence matched by the compassionate and appreciative holding of others. It also requires the vulnerability of knowing one is never fully sufficient without the other, and compassion towards oneself for one's status of "still becoming." Other ways exist, of course, which still get the job done, at least in the short term, but my experience would suggest that, over time, inauthentic behavior will expose the shortfalls in any relationships and work, leading to a habit of short-term runs which are over before they demand too much, and so their success is never tested in the fire of time. The habit is most easily described as a form of serial monogamy for someone who "shall laugh, but not all of your laughter, and weep, but not all of your tears," as Kahlil Gibran put it in *The Prophet*.

In truth, some of us are built for long runs, some of us not. Some of us get bored too easily and need more external variety of stimulation than others who thrive on stability, the known, and the reliable. As a culture we have a habit of falsely judging between these two, which is a shame. The invitation is to know oneself and be honest about oneself *before* we enter into relationships which presume different levels of commitment over time. Unfortunately, we can often only learn which style works best for us by trying them out in real time.

QUESTIONS FOR REFLECTION

1. To what extent do you feel that you have had to "learn on the job," and now wish to get training for the challenges for which you've had to improvise solutions?

2. Do you feel unsupported in your ministry? If so, where might you find others (volunteers or paid) to be part of your team to support and challenge you to be the next edition of yourself?

3. Do you have any diva or divo tendencies? (Most solo professionals do.) Who helps you laugh at yourself and become grounded in the moment when you work?

4. What are your experiences of great moments in your ministry? What went into making them happen? What can you continue to learn from them?

Epilogue

What did you learn? What would you have changed? Did it kill you? No? Moving on...

I HAVE LEFT PARISHES after several years of ministry, and I have left theater companies after many months of rehearsals and performances. In both we've grown close, because we've laughed and cried together, discovered new ideas, and been vulnerable together. We've loved and yet also disagreed, made mistakes, and seen miracles happen when words become not just flesh but spirit too.

Leavings create a deep and complicated mix of emotions, little deaths along with relief and, hopefully, excitement about potential new beginnings. At the center are the transitions of relationships which, regardless of everyone's best intentions, or at least polite words, will change and be reshaped if not completely ended. The invitation to "don't be a stranger" is rarely fulfilled in the following years.

At one parish where I worked for six years, we had a new transitional deacon for nine months each year (on the way for ordination as a priest), and I remember a parishioner once saying, "It's so hard to say goodbye. We grow to love them and care about them. They're so young and just starting out, and then they leave, and we have to start getting to know and help another and end up loving a new one all over again. It takes a toll."

I've also known theater companies where people who have been speaking words of love and anger to each other for months on stage will find it hard to suddenly have no avenue for the feelings once the performances are over, needing to channel such emotions in a new direction. (It's true; one's real life and a character's fictional life do sometimes overlap.)

Also true is that times will occur when one thinks, "Thank the Lord that's over!" and will need to heal from a choice to be part of an endeavor which didn't fulfill its promise, at least in some eyes. A sense of failure and wasted energy and time is not unknown. Yet the opposite is also true. Suddenly we have more time, fewer commitments, and possibilities for new horizons.

This book has been largely about the communications and relationships which we as working performers, presiders, and preachers make with others, but we should also be aware of the communication we've received over the time working, both from ourselves and from others. We aren't the same person at the end of the "run" as we were at the beginning, for better or for worse. And yes, that reference to the traditional marriage vow is deliberate. We've been in a covenantal relationship with an "other," both individually and communally, for all that time, be it through an author or The Author, human or Divine, and with casts as well as multiple audiences/congregations.

Our job of being a communicator required us to be in relationships, with an openness to change as a requirement to honor each one. And while we so often think we're changing "them," the truth is that "they" are also changing us. The change can't be avoided. The mere action of doing our work, even if we plan to remain unmoved or affected by it, will confirm or challenge our internal barriers, making any future "breakthrough" to a relational self that much easier or harder work. Someone who starts cut-off or aloof may stay and end the run that way, just further into their isolation, having dug their hole deeper with their own words and choices. I'm reminded of a line from a poem I read many years ago: "We build the walls of the self high, not to keep the horrors of the world out, but the terrors of the self in." I've known such poor souls; indeed, I've been one of them too.

All of which is really just a way of saying that at the end of a show's run, or a liturgical year, or when leaving a post, is a good, indeed wonderful opportunity for some reflection, both of oneself and what one needs from others. The ending is a chance for some analysis and evaluation of the experience, of what's been learned, of successes and failures. Unfortunately, also a sense of death and bereavement manifests. As such, I strongly suggest we use the services of someone who knows us, be it a wise friend, a professional therapist, or a spiritual director.

The fundamental reality of our work, both in the theater and in church, is to engage with incarnation. We're called to engage deeply and whole-heartedly, (indeed whole-bodily!) with what it means to have a body in the world with breath, a mind, an intellect, and emotions, and then use them on the journey of ministry and life. All these things are affected by words and gestures, with feelings and ideas.

The good news is that in both worlds one has easy, if not scientific, access to some raw data about what people thought of what you did and said. This includes applause (polite and genteel or loud and enthusiastic) and words of appreciation (from "thank you, that was nice" to "OMG, I need to go and have a stiff drink and think about that!"), as well as disagreement or disappointment (which usually doesn't make it as far as our earshot, for those folks generally just walk away). Mind you, when those less-than-happy messages can be delivered, we should hear them as gifts, even while also carefully deciding if they're valid or not.

Actors, people often say, have very thin skin (not true in my experience, though maybe I'm confusing their "skin" with their ego), and they commonly don't read reviews. However, someone should read them and filter what is useful back to those involved, both the affirmative and the learning points. Church communities sometimes have self-appointed critics who let the staff know what they think, which is also not helpful unless filtered through an independent "other" for validity. I remember one priest (not me) being verbally attacked (not for the first time) outside church after one Sunday's homily because the social implications of the gospel he preached (feed the hungry, clothe the poor, welcome the immigrant, etc.) did not match this person's political agenda. After listening patiently to the diatribe of the offended parishioner, he calmly replied, "And what does your therapist think about all that?" Incarnation has its challenges!

While most other arts and forms of communication have a layer in between the creative person and the receiver (the printed page, a canvas, the photographic process, some fabric), performers such as actors, musicians, ministers, and dancers are working with their own actual body and their own actual breath. Preachers are also usually working with their own actual ideas and revelations too. The level of vulnerability is huge. This is why the level of training and ongoing support needs to be extensive and thorough, enabling both the body and the breath to be at the service of the message, the communication, and the art.

Just like performance artists and other communicators, as a novice a new minister says the words, plays the notes, or dances the steps. The experienced person says, plays, or dances the feeling and intention behind and within the words, the music, or the steps, whatever's in the subtext. This is where the meaning lives. We can very often discover if we've touched this level of artistry by the responses we receive from others of where our words or steps have taken them or failed to take them. And to be clear, we can't control that, nor should we want to. We're opening a door for them to go on a journey in their own time and space. The journey is their own; we're just the ones who try to open the door. We cannot, of course, take all the credit either, for that must be shared with the author of the script, the composer and lyricist of the music, or the choreographer of the dance. But we're the ones who take those gifts off the page or imagination and make them present for a particular group at a particular time.

When Jesus said, "Whoever listens to you listens to me and whoever rejects you rejects me; and whoever rejects me rejects the One who sent me" (Lk. 10:16), he was challenging us not just to parrot back words we've learned but to be a new incarnation for the meaning we've experienced. Jesus didn't spend hours giving theological diatribes (except in John's gospel, and he almost certainly never said most of that, amazing as it is). Instead, he used simple phrases such as "be healed," "stand up," "don't be afraid," phrases too simple to be misunderstood yet so complex as to be earth-shattering in their consequences, like love. Phrases like these are what I mean by doorways to journeys which our audiences and congregations want to go through and on, if they can find the entry point and courage to continue.

These "doorway" moments are in many ways hidden in plain sight most of the time. Some combination of great skill and dumb luck is required to let them be revealed to others, often without us knowing we've done anything at all. Or, if we did think we did something, it was, in my experience, something completely different, as when you spend hours preparing a homily which is well received, but the first person who speaks about it reveals that they've taken something away from it that you had no idea you'd said.

As the Buddhists teach, "do the right thing and let go of the outcome." Our job is to create or choose the script and/or express it to the best of our ability and understanding. Our work is to try to keep getting better at our job. Leave the rest to others. Most importantly, we must remember that we aren't the doorway but are delivering an invitation to find and enter the doorway. In our Christian iconography, that is Jesus. (Jn.10:7)

This can be very hard for some to understand, both in the church and the theater. When one adds to that the fact that positions of community leadership tend to isolate the post holder, then the personal challenges get magnified. Significant personal maturity—and humility—is necessary to recognize that one is actually quite good at the job, but also not think one is indispensable or the only one so gifted.

Let's remind ourselves of the "Four Stages of Competence" for learning new skills:[1]

We begin with "Unconscious Incompetence," as when someone attempts, with no training, to do something for the first time, often thinking, "How hard could it be?" For example, a child's first painting, or someone's first attempt at singing "Let It Go" from *Frozen* at karaoke night, not knowing just how high that song gets.

Reality soon sets in, and we become, "Consciously Incompetent." During this period we know we're no Picasso or Taylor Swift, but we want to improve. Depending on the insecurity of the person, the degree of natural talent, and the giftedness of a teacher, this stage might continue for a longer or a shorter period.

At some point, however, we get to be good enough to confidently claim the name of the skill we're working on, though we're still aware we have things to learn and improve. This is the period of "Conscious Competence." Affirmations not only from friends but also strangers begin to sink in, and our confidence builds.

Finally, we reach a level of "Unconscious Competence" when we can undertake projects in our chosen field with enough knowledge that we can face standard problems unphased, and know where to go for assistance for the unique challenges. One might even become a leader in the field, and certainly a peer of recognized leaders. We are a "natural," even if we did a heck of a lot of work to get here. We have become just who we are.

This process applies equally to artists, plumbers, writers, electricians, dressmakers, preachers, presiders, and theater directors, to name but a few.

---

1. From the 1960 textbook *Management of Training Programs* by three management professors at New York University.

I remember a sports coach saying that they always try to balance their students' games by scheduling a couple against peers (at the same competence level) and then one against a team a couple of steps higher. Only by playing the slightly better students do the beginners improve. This is easier to implement in competitive sports than in the more solo activities of the stage or church. These worlds require feedback and coaching, and, as always, time and practice. (The old joke about someone being in New York and asking a cab driver, "How do I get to Carnegie Hall?" comes to mind. [A: "Practice, practice, practice!"])

One of the realities for student actors is that they take as many opportunities to see experienced actors work as they can, and to study with them in workshops and master classes. Similarly, dancers, singers and other musicians will do this too. I was watching an episode of *The Voice* recently on TV and two of the coaches (singers John Legend and "supercoach" Wynona Judd) both referenced their coaches and how they had helped them deal with specific problems in their performances. Professional athletes have physical trainers as well as psychologists on retainer to get their mind "online" for a difficult game. Professional dancers take daily classes right up to retirement (and sometimes beyond) to keep in shape. What do most preachers and presiders do for continuing education and feedback in their primary function? Where do they, (where do you) go to see examples of "best practice" and "new developments in our field?"

Many artists and athletes at the "Unconsciously Competent" level make sure they have at least one person from whom they are willing to hear the truth, and with whom they can discuss any problems and personal concerns, including physical and mental health issues. In most professional fields the practitioners are striving for excellence. While sports may focus on winning, most in the arts are aware that, for example, just because one singer is very popular, it doesn't mean no others are. Even if one actor is popular, plenty of work exists for many excellent others. The arts are not a zero-sum game. Excellence is celebrated, and the more the better.

While church is also not a zero-sum game, I fear those who work in its various manifestations don't get the training and support they need. They're doing the best they can with the training they've had and the examples they've witnessed. But most of them have gotten very little of even that, let alone ongoing support and review on a weekly or even monthly basis. Most parishioners are grateful for anything above basic competence, given prevailing standards. However, that's not enough for the nones and the next generation of seekers. Personally I think a congregation deserves as much as an audience when it comes to skill development and expertise. Abraham Herschel's words ring out again.

THAT WAS "GREAT!"

There's a difference between a great actor and a great performance. Similarly, great presiders and preachers may abound, but then there are occasions when a service, due to the skills of a whole team planning together, including the presider or preacher's leadership, "works," hitting all the right notes. Great moments for a performer, presider, or preacher all carry within themselves a combination of raw talent, hard work, life experiences, vision, and ultimately a surrender to the author. They've grown enough to understand the job, the skills they have at their disposal, and the work necessary to deliver the best of themself. A great actor, presider, or preacher would never rely on *ex opere operato* or its equivalent. Such reliance might be true—indeed, it must be true—but I believe we're called to work as if it weren't.

For those of us who know we aren't great, even though we may have had some amazing moments along the way, we know we're grateful for the truth of this ancient Latin phrase, even as we challenge ourselves to be better next time, for the sake of the people, audience, and/or congregation. In this way we can honor the author appropriately who, we hope, has given us a great gift by their words.

However . . .

I remember a comedian once quoting Shakespeare's *Twelfth Night* where Malvolio reads in a letter: "Some are born great, some achieve greatness, and some have greatness thrust upon them" (Act II Scene 5). To which the comedian added, "The rest of us have to put up with the miserable buggers."

Greatness is a severe threat to humility, which is the most necessary virtue for ministry, and indeed for one's spiritual life. The unhealed or unchallenged ego is the ever-present and energetic yet unhealthy driver to greatness for most of us: "I want to be good, even great at my job; and I want people, especially people I respect, to notice." This drive may never be voiced, or even noticed, but it's almost always present. This challenge is particularly great for those who have a new crowd every show, actors and traveling preachers alike. A presider in a stable community will frequently, over time, be challenged by this reality too.

A healthy ego is necessary for individuation and the ability for self-reflection and personal growth. A healthy ego gives a necessary sense of "self" against which one can explore the words and ideas of the "other," as opposed to projecting one's issues onto them. A healthy stimulus to the dialogue between "I" and "thou" was at the heart of Martin Buber's seminal book by the same name, published in 1923.[2] If the work is to "make the word(s) flesh," and I'm inviting another's word(s) to take residence in my flesh, even for a limited time, then I need to know where "I" ends and the "thou" of the author begins.

The hymn lyric (paraphrasing Gal 2:20) "I live, no 'tis not I who live but Christ who lives in me" might or might not be appropriate for one called to be a prophet, but it's not a recommended work aim for anyone else. Such an aim would, as it were, be taking Method acting a step too far. I do not believe we are called to merge with or be subsumed by the Beloved. I believe that the Beloved wishes us to transform into the fullness which is the living Christ within us, our own, unique fullest self.

Trust the Author. All the questions which come up will find their answer in the script. Surrender to it.

---

2. Martin Buber. *I and Thou* 1923

Appendix

EXAMPLE ONE

A homily in the medium of storytelling by a character in the story.

Palm Sunday: Grandpa Donkey's Tale

You must remember I was much younger when all this happened, even though to me it seems like it was just yesterday. My favorite story growing up had been the one about the ending of the war between the humans and the rest of creation. The war had been going on for longer than anyone could remember, and no one really knows how it started.

For the longest time all the animals, and birds and fish, and even the plants, the rocks and stones had been living in fear, fear of humans and the way they treated the rest of us. Don't get me wrong, I know we are not perfect, and we donkeys sometimes play the fool more than most, but the humans were created in God's image, so we expected more from them.

We thought they were the ones called to be good stewards of the world, bringing hope to all for the rebuilding of the Garden of Eden, where everything is balanced, just as God intended. My mother used to tell me stories about how, one day, a person would be born who understood us, the created world of animals, plants and stones. Someone who would not be afraid of the desert or the mighty waters, who could see the beauty in the flowers of the field, and freedom in the birds of the air. And they would reconcile all creation. And he or she would arrive, not riding on the back of an eagle, not in some great chariot drawn by horses or zebras or elephants but riding on the back of a young donkey.

"Just like you" she would say.

Now there had been a lot of talk about 30 years ago, when my great grandad had walked the journey from Nazareth to Bethlehem. To his dying day he maintained that the pregnant woman he carried on that journey was like no other person he had ever had to carry. Everyone laughed at him, of course, for sounding so grand, and you know how much we donkeys like to laugh! He said she was like carrying "a porcelain jar of delicate flowers." He was a bit of a poet, my great granddad!

He had been there when the woman had given birth, along with some other animals, and they had all agreed that it was so special that maybe the war between the humans and the rest of the world might be coming to an end. But nothing came of it. The war didn't stop. But that didn't stop us believing the story that one day it would.

The day we are talking about, mother and I had been left tied up to the rail at the edge of the village. This was unusual as mother was normally taken to the fields and I was left at home, being too young yet to go to work. I was excited!

I'd never seen the streets before, the people bustling about with baskets and jars. The stallholders were calling out their wares. Men and women were arguing, as usual, about the price and the quality of the produce to get the best deal. The noise was really loud—and they say us donkeys make a racket! We'd not been there long when three men walked up, untied the rope and led us away. We walked up the hill, away from the noise. I asked my mother where we were going, but she said just to be quiet, and everything would be alright.

She sensed the men were friendly, though I could see she was a little nervous, looking back a lot to see if we were being followed. But apparently everything had been arranged before. In a clearing just off the road a small crowd was gathered. We were led into the middle and some cloaks were spread on our backs. A man came up, holding some grass in his hand, which he fed to my mother. She ate it and then nuzzled his arm, something I'd never seen her do before. Then he moved to me, running his hand across my nose and cheek, down my neck and let it rest at the base of my mane.

I suppose I should have been frightened, but somehow, I trusted him. With the help of one of the others he mounted me and, for the first time in my life, I was carrying someone! It wasn't at all like I had expected from all the stories I had heard from the older donkeys, of how people put great weights on our backs, or of how people sat very heavily, sometimes causing us to stumble forward rather than walk properly.

He held himself like a king, straight backed, but not stiff, upright, but not proud. He sat with me, not just on me.

"Jerusalem" he said, and my mother nodded, so I started off, down the other side of the hill, towards the huge city in the distance.

From the moment we came into view of the city, the crowd walking with us grew and grew. The noise and excitement was again like nothing I had ever heard before. People shouted and cheered; they waved palm branches taken from the nearby trees. Some people even spread their cloaks on the ground for us to walk on, my mother and I.

I felt like a king! But that was not all.

The trees themselves seemed to be waving, and the stones beneath my hooves were whispering and calling out "this is the one, this is him, the war is over! Peace at last!"

And it was then that I began to understand why it was so easy to carry my first rider. Soon we were inside the city walls, with its narrow streets. People looked out of their windows and from the roofs of their houses, waving anything they could lay their hands on, cloths, aprons, even the washing! It was only then that I saw that not all the people were cheering. Some looked worried, and even angry.

I was surprised. Why did they have to ask, "who is it?" Couldn't they hear the trees and the stones calling out over the noise of the crowd? Were they not expecting their messiah, their savior too?

Eventually we reached a large open space near a big building which sat on the top of the hill. Mother stopped walking, so I did too.

The man got off, walked in front of me, and pulled from his tunic a handful of the sweetest grass I have ever eaten, and fed it to me. A young boy came up and took the rope from the man and began to lead us back to our village as the man walked up to the steps to the great building and began talking to the huge crowd that was quickly gathering.

As we went away, we nearly ran into a column of soldiers marching towards the square. I remember my mother saying she hoped they were not going to arrest the man. I laughed and said: "Of course they won't, because he's the Messiah!"

She looked at me with wide eyes and asked: "Whatever made you say that?"

"Well, he is, isn't he?" I asked back.

"Yes, I think he is," she smiled.

We walked back the rest of the way in silence and, although we've talked of it often since, none of the other animals at the farm seemed to understand or believe our story.

Like my great granddad before me telling his story of the walk from Nazareth to Bethlehem, I've told my story of the walk to Jerusalem to my children and my other great-grandchildren before you. They like it a lot, but I'm not sure they believe that I really carried the Messiah.

But I do!

In fact, I know I did, and that therefore the war IS ended. Or at least it should be.

I suppose there's a chance that those soldiers we saw did arrest the man and stopped him talking. But surely the people wouldn't have let them do that, would they? They would have protected him, don't you think? After all, surely they wanted the war to end as much as we do, right? They wanted the Messiah to come and bring peace, didn't they?

Oh well, I'm going to keep telling the story in the hope that some folks will believe.

After all, if I don't tell the story and keep the hope alive, who will?

EXAMPLE TWO

A one-sided telephone conversation

"If it causes you to offend, cut it off."

(Readings: Mk. 9:38–48.)

(dialing on phone) 1-800—4 HEAVEN
(Hums or sings along to a popular hymn tune while waiting. Someone answers.)
Hello!
Oh yes, er, of course. And also with you. *(pause)*
Yes, I wondered if I could talk with someone about today's gospel reading please? Might St. Mark be available? *(pause)*
Oh, that's unfortunate. Maybe someone else who was around when he was writing? *(pause)*
Oh you can, that's great! So, really, you were around then, were you? *(pause)*

APPENDIX

Wow!! May I ask, what's your name? (*pause* and *wide-eyed surprised look!*)

Yes, sorry Lord, I didn't recognize your voice. (*pause*)

I suppose you do. And I'm sorry to disturb you, especially on a Sunday. You must be exhausted after a full day of worldwide church! (*pause*)

Yes, you and Father Christmas, just Alaska, Hawaii and the Pacific Islands left. (*pause*)

Well, thanks for always dropping in. It wouldn't be the same without you! (*pause*)

And everyone says hi back! (*pause*)

I'll tell . . . (*name of music leader*)—it's one my favorites songs too, people seem to like it. (*pause*)

So, my call, yes. Gosh I feel rather silly actually asking you this question, I hope you don't mind. (*pause*)

Well, today's gospel reading, it sort of goes all over the place, so I was wondering, if it's not too rude to ask, were you ever diagnosed with a split personality disorder? (*pause*)

Thank you, I was afraid it was just me! (*pause*)

So why did Mark put it all together like that? I mean, I hope you didn't want us to take that second bit literally? (*pause*)

Phew! Because that would have been a real problem! (*pause*)

Well I suppose the reason we don't have a problem with the *first* bit is, and I haven't taken a vote or anything, but I think I can guess that everyone here doesn't think God as Creator can ever be limited, not even within you as God's child. I hope that's alright. I mean, wisdom can't be contained, right? God's voice always finds a way out. (*pause*)

Erm, . . . I think Balaam's talking donkey is my favorite example, from the Book of Numbers. (*pause*)

I'm sure you did! It's certainly very popular in Sunday Schools! (*pause*)

Examples for me would include the Buddha, who seemed to have a lot of very wise things to say about living an ethical life. And then there's all the great 12-Step programs around that help people. And of course, the healing ministries of various charismatic ministers and groups across the world, along with the whole medical and therapeutic professions. (*pause*)

You're right—I forgot about a parent kissing a hurt or bruise better. A frequent miracle. (*pause*)

Yes, but that's what makes the second part of the gospel so difficult to hear. (*pause*)

What could you—or Mark—or was it Peter's idea, since we think it was him who was telling the story to Mark anyway, . . . what could any of you hope to possibly achieve by adding that part? I mean, people have taken it literally and have cut off body parts in the past—and not just hands and feet! (*pause*)

What do you mean "symbolically"? (*pause*)

Er . . . a hand symbolizes . . . er . . . what I do? I do things with my hands. (*pause*)

And, er . . . I walk with my feet, so I go in certain directions literally—and yes, fine, symbolically too. (*pause*)

My eyes? Well, I suppose one could say that **how** I choose to see things, the perspective or lens I put on facts, can change what I see. I'm not sure what you're getting at in this case. (*pause*)

Ah yes, as in seeing through the experience of my privilege or prejudice, even my wealth, I'm not really seeing the truth. (*pause*)

But I've been working really hard not to do any of those! You know, to get over my in-built privilege AND prejudice and stuff! (*pause*)

Okay. Noted! I will try harder! (*pause*)

But why didn't you just say that, rather than this really violent stuff? (*pause*)

I'm not sure expecting humans to work a little to get into the meaning is a good idea! (*pause*)

You might trust us, but I certainly wouldn't! (*pause*)

Yes, I suppose you're right, people do remember it more easily that anything that sounds like New Age psychobabble. (*pause*)

Apologies. You're right, New Age psychobabble wasn't around when Mark was writing. I take your point. (*pause*)

Er, . . . yes, . . . actually, that does indeed answer my questions. It seems I'm the one with the split-personality disorder. It's like St. Paul wrote about himself: I have the me I think I am in my head, who is basically kind of nice, but then there's the real one who lives in the world and, even when I try not to be, is kind of judgmental and wrapped up in my own comforts and self-importance. (*pause*)

Er, yes, . . . that did sound kind of like a confession, didn't it. Can you forgive me? (*pause*)

Thank you. So, what's my penance? (*pause*)

My choice? (*pause*)

Okay, so this week I will try harder to ensure that my hands only do justice,

... that my feet only walk humbly

... and that my eyes see your love in all your creation. (*pause*)

I appreciate that, but you do realize that I probably won't be very successful at it. I mean, old habits die hard. (*pause*)

"Cut them off." I should've seen that coming, shouldn't I! Okay! I'll see what I can do. (*pause*)

Thank you—and yes, it's always amazing to talk to you too. (*pause*)

Sure. (*to congregation*) He sends his love and says . . . (*name of parishioner who recently died*), arrived safely, and he's watching over . . . (*name or two of those sick or suffering, or* "those on the prayer list".)

Give our love to Hawaii!

'Bye.

Bibliography

Anderson, H., and Edward Foley. *Mighty Stories, Dangerous Rituals.* San Francisco: Jossey-Bass, 1998.
Brook, Peter. *The Empty Space.* New York: Simon & Schuster, 1996.
Countryman, L. William. *Living on the Border of the Holy.* Harrisburg: Morehouse, 1999.
Driver, Tom F. *The Magic of Ritual.* San Francisco: HarperCollins, 1991.
Gibran, Kahlil. *The Prophet.* West Molesey, UK: Senate, 2003.
Haight, Roger. *Spiritual AND Religious.* Maryknoll, NY: Orbis, 2016.
Herschel, Abraham Joshua. *God in Search of Man: A Philosophy of Judaism.* New York: Farrar, Strauss and Giroux, 1976.
Hovda, Robert W. *Strong, Loving and Wise.* Minnesota, Liturgical, 1976.
Howe, E. Graham. *She and Me.* London: Triton, 1974.
Jefferts Schori, Katherine. *Gathering at God's Table.* Woodstock: SkyLight Paths, 2012.
Johnson, Todd E., and Dale Savidge. *Performing the Sacred.* Grand Rapids: Baker Academic, 2009.
Martos, Joseph. *Honest Ritual, Honest Sacraments.* Eugene OR: Resource Publications, 2017.
Moltmann, Jurgen. *Theology of Play.* New York: Harper & Row, 1972.
Nouwen, Henri J. M. *The Wounded Healer.* New York: Knopf Doubleday, 1972.
Orobator, Agbonkhianmeghe E., ed. *The Church We Want.* Maryknoll: Orbis, 2016.
Rahner, Karl. *Karl Rahner's Writings on Literature, Music and the Visual Arts* Translated by Gesa E. Thiessen. London: Bloomsbury, 2021.
Riso, Don Richard, and Russ Hudson. *The Wisdom of the Enneagram.* New York: Bantam, 1999.
Rosmini, Antonio. *The Five Wounds of the Church.* Translated by H. P. Liddon. London UK: Rivingtons, 1883.
Royal National Theatre. *Platform Papers: 6. Peter Brook.* London, UK: Royal National Theatre 1994.
Spong, John Selby. *A New Christianity for a New World.* San Francisco; HarperCollins, 2001.
Turner, Victor. *From Ritual to Theatre.* New York: Performing Arts Journal, 1982.
United States Catholic Conference. *Environment and Art in Catholic Worship.* Chicago: Liturgical Training, 1986.

www.ingramcontent.com/pod-product-compliance
Lightning Source LLC
Chambersburg PA
CBHW072127160426
43197CB00012B/2027